The Wiccan Way

By the same author

The Wiccan Path, published in the UK as *Hedge Witch*
Lamp of the Goddess formerly published as *Reincarnation and the Dark Goddess*

The Wiccan Way

Magical Spirituality for the Solitary Pagan

RAE BETH

Illustrations by
Poppy Palin

PHOENIX PUBLISHING INC.

PHOENIX PUBLISHING INC.
P.O. Box 3829
Blaine, Washington USA 98231
www.phoenixpublishing.com

Published in the U.K.
as *The Hedge Witch's Way* by
ROBERT HALE LTD.
45-47 Clerkenwell Green
London EC1R 0HT

ISBN 0-919345-95-6

Cover design by Richard Bakker

Printed in the USA

This book is dedicated to my familiar spirits
And to my wise husband, Ashley
And to my mother, Ellen, a natural mystic

Contents

Introduction

Here is a guide to the spirituality which lies behind the practice of solitary witchcraft. It is a magical spirituality because, to a witch, the boundaries between this world and the spirit realm are not firm. A mystical appreciation of spirit in all things is what makes a witch. So this book is for all the natural mystics – the hedge witches, as they are sometimes called. It describes practices which are far simpler than those in my earlier book, *The Wiccan Path*, at least in technical terms. There is much less reliance on magical equipment and ritual and much more on magical prayer and upon inner journeying with our familiar spirits.

It may seem strange that a second book upon the subject of solitary witchcraft should deal with what is less complex than what went before. However, by one of those paradoxes so common in magic, it is true that the 'inner courts' of our tradition are less full of procedure, formality and so on – and more to do with our psychic experience and our spirituality.

The full formal rituals described in *The Wiccan Path* can still be very rewarding to enact. By learning the skills of wild-wood mysticism (as our inner knowledge may be called), we can come to them with an increased psychic strength and understanding.

All the ideas in this book are drawn from traditional knowledge about the practice of traveling 'between the worlds', and of relating to deities or spirits from middle Earth, the underworld or the upperworld. Such knowledge is, indeed, at the root of the tree of witchcraft. And when these techniques are allied with everyday tasks or simple ritual acts, we can help to bring back the lost magic to the world and to close the rift between the beautiful otherworld and our own, to the healing of all beings.

The book starts, pedestrianly enough, with a long look at the practice of Pagan prayer, as used by witches. Stay with it and it will fly you to other realms.

Bright Blessings

Rae Beth
Samhain – 2000
Bath

1 Prayer and Enchantment

This book is for anyone who wants to follow a spiritual way, and to work natural magic in a style that is powerful and yet informal, like a wild wood; to be a witch who is a natural mystic, and to work alone, solitary, independent of covens, practicing a living witchcraft that comes from an awareness of the spirits of nature, and that arises as naturally as a spring from the earth.

Such a witchcraft does not need a complex, intellectual knowledge of the past practices of witches in many lands, rewarding though such a study may be. It is immediate, direct and rooted in a feeling for the symbolic, poetic, spiritual aspects of Earth. What it does need is a sound grasp of the basic principles of magic. This I have called 'hedge witchcraft', and if it is to be more than an adjunct to other spiritual practices, it must come from experience of deep communion with Goddesses and Gods of Pagan realms. This I have called the 'wildwood mysticism'. From such an experience can unfold a real sense of spiritual guidance, such as is known by many people living in the remnants of tribal cultures, worldwide. This knowledge, for today's Europeans, is based in our own Pagan traditions and direct revelation. It underpins the meaning of witchcraft and gives the witch inner strength.

Becoming a wildwood mystic is not difficult at all. It just needs a sense of the sacred, when faced with nature's tides within the land we are standing on. Whether we see mother

– and father – nature as awesome, threatening, beautiful, threatened, or all of these! An attitude of worship, when sensing mysteries inherent in the rocks, trees, springs and hills and wild creatures. Therefore, at the most simple level, this book is about witches' prayers.

Why are such prayers so important? Well, they are the easiest way to a profound experience. Not only do they open our spirits to awareness of the deities, but also help us to be in the state of mind in which we can link with familiars and spirit guides. And, to put it straightforwardly, there is no method which is more simple to enable us to transcend the everyday world and be in connection with psychic dimensions and realms of spirit. Pagan prayers, as said by witches, can make psychic and spiritual perceptions of nature come easily, thus creating a real foundation for a wildwood mysticism. This is because Pagan prayers, quite simply, attune our spirits to purely Pagan realms of nature and ancient wisdom.

Any one of the examples given in this book can be used as it stands, or altered to suit your needs – or discarded, having been used as a seed idea for your own fresh attempts. Toward the end, I will explain how to create your own entirely new ones, whenever you need to.

There are prayers for all purposes e.g. for things like healing, finding love, gaining in magical strength, coming into harmony with fate, contacting a familiar spirit and celebrating the eight sabbats of the witch's year.

For witches, distinctions between prayers and spells can fade quickly, so the prayers are magical in themselves, as well as being the foundation for magic ritual. This is to do with the way they are worded, and also with the nature of the witches' deities. Witches see the Goddesses and Gods as possessing a continuum of powers and qualities, ranging from the elemental (as expressed in a storm, forest, a stag's fertility, hunger, the physical effects of the Moon, instinctual route finding, etc.) to the most divine (like love, compassion, beauty, truth, strength or natural justice). Those whom we worship encompass both the raw powers of nature and all her possibilities of psychic, spiritual and moral harmony, such as those expressed in mother love, the playfulness of a dolphin, heroic courage and the intricacies of a Mozart symphony. Unlike the world's mainstream faiths, Paganism does not define goodness as distinct from nature, but as contained within or arising from it, like a crystal from rock.

It is this inclusiveness of both ends of the spectrum – raw power and transcendent wisdom – that marks a witch's understanding of the Goddesses and Gods and characterizes a witch's prayer, giving to such prayers a power of connection between the physical and psychospiritual dimensions of life, thus making them magically effective. This is not to say that a witch glorifies all instinctive behavior, even when it is cruel. Rather, we find nature's cruelty innocent. It is the cruelty of those who are advanced enough (in consciousness) to make a choice which is really a straying from divine will. Pagan deities urge us to an increase in wisdom, and of all awareness.

If you had thought, or even hoped, to find a witch's mystical knowledge to be a way of invoking raw power, with no particular rules about kindliness, then read no further. Wildwood mysticism develops a sense of responsibility toward all beings, beginning with the spirits of the land itself, encompassing the balance of nature and including other people. All this makes a witch's prayers challenging, alive and developmental, considering that they are often also concerned with achieving specific goals. And if we make mistakes, we have to pay. This is not to say that there is some kind of karmic debt-or-credit book in the sky, kept for witches, by the Moon Goddess or Horned God! It is just that it is impossible to work magic without (eventually, in some way) becoming involved with the consequences.

I think it is the Buddhists who say 'Be careful of what you

ask for. You might get it.' A witch would add, 'When it comes to spells, you'll get what goes into the package along with what you wanted.' And you'll eventually be on the receiving end of whatever energy you have invoked, but amplified. 'What goes around comes around.' We call this the Law of Threefold Return. It is the same idea as in the line 'You reap as you sow.'

Despite fears or possible misunderstandings, the new witch-craft is popular nowadays. Most people have heard of it, and many who would have had difficulty in finding their own kind of spirituality are now heaving a big sigh of relief and saying, 'So that's it. That's what I am. I've come home to myself at last. I am some kind of witch/wisewoman/shaman/wildwood mystic. I have my spiritual path, at last.' Letters I have received from all over Britain and America, such joyful letters, attest to this.

But rituals of the Craft can sometimes seem intimidating because they are too complex for the beginner, or too long. Lighting a candle or two, and saying a witch's prayer, is as simple as you can get. Even when followed by spellcasting procedures, this is not too daunting. And yet it is powerful, magical and fruitful if approached in the spirit of the wild-wood mystic.

Even for the seasoned witch, simplicity can be refreshing. It can produce the effect of a new and uncluttered start, a clean page; the chance to rethink the way, what it means, how to develop it for the times that we live in; the chance to forget preconceived ideas, just to start from a most simple thing – Pagan prayer – and see what happens.

As the poet Tennyson said, 'More things are wrought by prayer than this world dreams of.'

2 Who Is It We're Praying To?

As I have said, witches' deities are the Pagan Goddesses and
Gods, who were worshiped by our ancestors. But the wildwood mystic needs to understand the term 'Pagan'. It means
'of the countryside', from the Latin Pagus (country district), and
implies beliefs formed from a contact with nature which arose
before modern cities, or industry, came to be. This does not
mean that city dwellers can't be Pagan, for nature is everywhere; we just have to look a bit harder for her in the city.
What it does mean is a religious faith in which nature is held to
be sacred, not just the abode of the spirit, but even the manifestation of it. Native American Paganism illustrates this
clearly. There is not a pool, tree, animal, bird or bee which
does not have its own intrinsic spiritual essence and thus its
particular natural wisdom, contributing to the balance of
nature. Here in Britain, our Native European ancestors
believed the same sorts of things, in this respect. And such
ideas are still alive today, in modern witchcraft and in all new
Paganism.

However, people were burned at the stake for Paganism in
the European past. Witches, druids, heathens of all kinds and
even Christian heretics were executed in large numbers, for
basing their beliefs and rites partly upon the sanctity of
nature, and/or for consulting with nature spirits or faeries (as
Joan of Arc did). Nowadays, it is safe (and legally protected)
to claim such beliefs again, and even more poignant and

meaningful to do so, now that no tree is safe from the developer's axe and no species is entirely safe from extinction. However, many people have been frightened off from having witchy beliefs by the legacy of the great persecution. So why did it happen?

Well, it had to do with the Christian Church's struggle to establish its own supremacy. It was deemed necessary to destroy the arch rival – that is, native European spirituality. All Pagans (and even Christian heretics) were threats to the Roman Catholic monopoly, with its drive toward absolute dominance in all religious beliefs and practices. This was explained as being for the good of all our souls. It also resulted in an extraordinarily large and powerful institution (with a great deal of money).

Another aspect of the burning times was the demonizing of all Pagan deities. Our Gods are supposed to be devils, our Goddesses evil. This message continues to be put across in books, films and anti-Pagan propaganda, to this day. Such a message might well put off anyone from praying to our Mother Earth, let alone to the Horned God, Cernunnos.

Let us be in no doubt about it, evil does exist. Anyone who has ever thought about the cruelty in this world knows there is no uncertainty about that. And it would be naïve to say that no Pagan ever did anything wrong. The ancient Pagan world held every kind of extreme, from the gentleness of the Isian priesthood, who practiced pacifism, vegetarianism and sexual abstinence, to the brutality of certain tribespeople, who practiced human sacrifice, and who were also often guilty of ill-wishing other people and laying curses. Unfortunately, the same thing has been true of Christianity. Animals have often been sacrificed, for sheer amusement, by many Christians: for instance, the destruction of the buffalo in North America. Humans have been sacrificed in unjust wars 'with God on our side', over and over again. Christianity has been made the rationale

17

for conquest of the heathen, and invasion and exploitation of other peoples' countries and natural resources. As already pointed out, there was the torture and sacrifice of Pagans and heretics, for the sake of the Church's supremacy, in the Middle Ages. All that this means, unfortunately, is that undeveloped human nature is much the same in any religious system. But it would be as absurd to blame the Pagan deities for this as it would be to blame Jesus for all the terrible things done in his name, or to blame Allah for Muslim fanaticism.

Come to think of it, some really evil things have been done by atheists, too. It would appear that no religion is exempt from this charge, and neither are the nonreligious.

In other words, evil cannot be overcome by denouncing Pagan deities, or destroying wildwood mysticism. Indeed, enormous damage – in environmental, human and cultural terms – has resulted from trying to do so. It is time, therefore, that witches' prayers began to be said again; high time that a wildwood mysticism be seen to be necessary, as well as wholesome. Therefore, let us look more closely at what Pagan deities are.

Kathy Jones, in her book *In the Nature of Avalon*, says the following: 'One of the glories of the Goddess is that she is mutable, ever changing, presenting different faces to each person who goes in search of her. She is one and she is many, and within each of the many the one is also to be found.' The same goes for the God. This clears up a potential source of confusion. For there may seem to be a quite bewildering multiplicity of Pagan Goddesses and Gods. This is partly because many different tribes, cultures and nations have had their own name for a Goddess of healing or a God of truth, for example. It is important to remember that, whatever their names or perceived powers, each Goddess or God is simply a resonance of the one Great Goddess, or Great God. This point is made most clearly in Egyptian mythology. For example, in the Heliopolitan Recension (the earliest collection of Egyptian funerary literature), where deities are described as sons and daughters, or grandsons, granddaughters etc. of the original mother and father.

But who are this Pagan mother and father in the first place? Perhaps the best way to describe them is as the spirit that runs through all things – creating, upholding, transforming, evolving life, in both its feminine aspect (the Goddess) and its masculine aspect (the God). They cannot be reduced to rational formulae, for they are mystery. Only a poem will do, or symbolism (as in any art form) to express the nature of Goddess or God.

For instance, we can say of the Great Goddess that she is the vision from which life uprises; she is a whisper of light, like white wings in darkness; she is the tranquility of a whale and also the ocean of deep space, primordial night. She is the Earth's dreaming self, with images like many-colored bright crystals. And she is the patient industry of worms, that keep the Earth healthy. And the life and joyfulness of every wild creature. And she is the elements, the voice of rivers and wildfire on the mountain, and wind that blows across Arctic wastes. And she is in silence. She is all time, when it lasts so long that one drop of water from a cave roof would measure a whole aeon. She is memory in a seed. She is the poem that keeps on being chanted in quietness. She is music from which each song arises. She is the continuum.

Life proceeds from all her dreaming, whether that is in the dreamspace of the womb, where a child is formed, or in the deep inner space of the soul, where each one of us may hold pure aspirations and visions. She is the sacred, the numinous, giving rise to meaning as well as to being.

She is also a wise love, an inclusiveness. She relates one creature and image to another. She holds all together and is

at the centre, and also around it all, containing. She is integration and synthesis, sustaining. She is the ground of all
being. Within the furthest star, within the Sun and Moon and
Earth and within our spirits.

By a strange paradox, she is not always found by turning
inward. She is also the stillness known beyond the wildest
dance and within sexual passion. And she is abundance, the
cornfields, the orchards, all forms of life. Whether we call her
Brigid, Isis, Mari-Morgan, Aradia, or by any other name, she
is eternal.

While she is at the heart of life, originator of existence, the
God's role is different. Not more nor less valuable, but not
the same. He is the great catalyst, the changer. He is inno-
vation, magician, experimenter on a cosmic scale. He is the
shock of life, working as a portent to disturb our settled
conclusions, saying, 'Let's try a new way.' He is trickster and
magus. He is prophecy, speaking from an oak tree. Life
cannot get too settled in the presence of the God, for he will
not allow it. He is a breath full of desire. And he is also paradox; ruthless in setting in motion inescapable change, and
demanding that we take risks, he is also the protector,
defending the helpless. He doesn't respect a lack of courage,
though he understands fear and honors a sensible prudence.
But he always says, 'Let's try a new step in the dance, a new
picture, another way of life. Come on, move! I can bring the
dream to reality in unexpected ways. Listen, I have a dream
too. It's of an adventure. For I am the faraway landscape, I
am the long journey. On the way, we will see and do all
you've ever imagined – but you'll have to be daring. I am the
dark beneath tree bark and the cave's phosphorescence and
the glint within the goat's eyes, as well as green leaves and
the sunlight and tenderness.'

He is all natural justice, the guardian of nature's balance –
yet also the sudden twist, the wild card, the unexpected. He

is both the wise man and the rebel who fights against the destruction of untamed places. And he is the wild places.

He is the sacred acrobat, he is playful. He is that power in all beings.

And whether we call him Manannan, Osiris, Bran, Robin or Cernunnos, or by any other name, he, too, is eternal.

In the end, they are each the sacred mystery, which cannot be constrained, contained or reduced. They are the essence of life and all meaning.

But there is a further way of understanding the mysteries, and different aspects of the deities, within wildwood mysticism. It is based upon shamanic beliefs. Please note, the word 'shamanism' has a very precise interpretation for academics and scholars, but I am merely using it here in its loose and popular sense: to imply tribal practices wherein a person – man or woman – would work with the spirits, undertaking trance journeys to meet them, in order to heal another person, plant, animal, place or situation.

Using the shamanic model, then, existence has three main divisions, or levels. These are the underworld, middle Earth and the upperworld, perceived as three aspects of an imagined world tree, around which all existence revolves, and all beings live out their lives. This tree, whose trunk is the axis of the universe, has been and still is a part of many Pagan traditions worldwide. In Britain, it is seen as an oak or an apple tree, as the Celtic ancestors deemed it. Or, because of our Nordic forebears, an ash tree. To the Chinese, it was a peach; to the Lakota Indians, a poplar. But the point about this world tree (whatever the species) is that it both delineates and links the three realms of existence. The underworld (life's roots and psychospiritual causes), middle Earth (mortal life in all its glory), the upperworld (life's aspirations.) The deities of each of these realms can be addressed over matters specific to their domain.

poppy palin

First, we will look at the underworld region. Here are the deities of water and therefore, the depths, profundity, as well as the roots of things, within the dark earth. This is the place from which all things grow, symbolically, and to which they return. It can be seen as both tomb and womb. A very watery place, it contains springs and underground streams and rivers and even oceans (for sea level is below land level) as well as rocks, stones, caves and the soil.

What nourishes and freshens life from its beginnings? What are the most basic causes of what happens? And what are our deepest feelings? All these things are within the underworld, for it sustains and shapes life from underneath. It is about whatever lies below the surface, the roots of all things, the causes. For this reason, it is said (in Celtic tradition) to be the home of those who weave the web of fate – the faeries. And it is not a dismal place. Underneath the land, within the hollow hills, or across the sea on magic islands, there is, traditionally, another dimension. It is a place of great magic and beauty, the faerie realm, and it underlies all existence. The underworld is the repository of what Eastern mystics might call 'karma' – the things we do which affect and shape our future. It is also the realm where our Pagan ancestors live, the spirits of the dead. All underworld deities therefore preside over fate and the changing or transforming of it, through magic. They are responsible for all hidden causes and deep motivations. They are also concerned with profound healing, and with issues of death and rebirth. We do not have to know any of their traditional names to invoke them, but can simply pray to them as Goddess and God of Fate and the Faerie Realms. They are known as the Dark Goddesses and Gods. This is not because they are in any way evil, but because their realm contains the subtle concealed things, the root causes.

The Goddesses and Gods of middle Earth are much more obvious. These are the deities of all abundant life, of the physical realm we live in. But their domain is not just that of appearances and our manifest bodies, but also of the spirits of all creatures, the nature spirits of rock and tree and hill and pool and fox and hawk and moth and frog and ourselves –

everything. Theirs is the realm in which ideas gain form and adventures are not just fantasies, but are lived, fully. They are the givers of what we need to survive, the full bowl and the laden table. It is not their will that some should have and some should not, for they value all, equally. Through them, our plans take on practical shape and creativity is manifested, and dreams come true. Unfortunately, so do nightmares, if what we have given, individually or collectively, to the underworld fate weavers, consists of dubious causes. However, the lady and lord of all middle Earth have a strong magic to rebalance nature, and our lives, if problems should arise. Their methods of doing so may not be what we'd have envisaged, or would have wished; they may even be ruthless, but they will always restore life's balance. They are, after all, the life force in its manifest form. They are nature's wisdom. If we honor them, we can have creative lives, fulfillment, undamaged skies, clean seas, real food, a just society, healthy technology. We can have a nonexploitative culture.

The area all around the trunk of this imagined world tree is that of middle Earth's deities. Everything that is above ground and beneath sky.

Up among the branches is the place of the upperworld Goddesses and Gods. Imagine peering up at the topmost leaves and twigs. Among them, we see the Sun shining or, at night, the Moon, stars and planets. Deities of these, the heavenly bodies, are all connected with cosmic tides and influences, as seen in astrology. Their influence is woven into the webs of fate by the faerie fate weavers, just as sun, moon or starlight are reflected in water. So they are the big picture, the universal perspective. From the upperworld deities, we can receive the highest aspirations and visions. Through them, we can rise above our fears and worries, and sense infinity. Failure to honor them can lead to blinkered lives and to much pettiness. They are the bestowers of a transcendence which helps us attain a greater understanding of life's possibilities, and allows us to see things in a much larger context. Despite the sometimes amoral behavior of Gods and Goddesses of planets and luminaries (which is something of a distortion, and not a true understanding of their natures), as depicted in Greek mythology, these are the deities who can inspire a nobility in our goals and our souls. Their influence in our lives only goes wrong when we fail to keep our feet on the ground while looking at them. Then we get out of touch with our reality and our common humanity. We learn that the shadow side of, say, Jupiter or Venus, or any supernatural power, can indeed be destructive but if we remember our psychic roots in the underworld, our lives upon middle Earth, our responsibilities, then we can pray to them for blessings. We then find that they give the sublime moments in life or in ourselves.

The above is what is meant by the world tree and the three realms of deities. To a hedge witch and wildwood mystic, a tree (any tree) will do to symbolize this. For it not only has the three distinct levels of roots, trunk and branches, but is, in fact, one entire entity – just like the Great Goddess or Great God, whose being is all things.

3 Addressing Mystery

Not so long ago, the stereotypical witch's prayer would be thought to run something like this: 'Great Demon, please give me lots of money. And the chance to go to bed with ___ I will kill three black hens and light black candles.' Or some variation on that theme.

Nowadays, it is recognized that non-Christian prayers, even witches' prayers, are not necessarily greedy or manipulative. Nevertheless, the subject of prayer is a loaded one. If you are a hedge witch or any other kind of Pagan, then you are clearly not praying to Jesus or the biblical God, but to the kind of deities described in the preceding chapter. Thanks, as I have said, to the legacy of the witch hunts, and today's cult of horror movies, this can still be regarded as a daring and possibly dangerous thing to do. It is as though people feel that a little mild use of magic is one thing, but actually praying to Pagan deities is a serious, religious, spiritual matter. It shows a genuine stepping outside of the Christian fold. The making of another religious commitment. Scary!

At the other end of the spectrum is a totally different reaction. To many people, prayer is associated with a sanctimonious smugness that is unpleasant. We have the Victorian Church to thank for this, along with present-day hypocrisy. Though most people do pray, in moments of crisis, piety is just not sexy. In fact, most people would rather be caught having sex in public than saying a prayer!

Perhaps these two problems might cancel each other out for those considering the path of the wildwood mystic? Pagan prayers are very reverent, but on the other hand (having a flash of rebellion and addressing the deities of nature) they are, indeed, sexy.

Joking apart, the aim of this book is to show how a wildwood mystic prays and how she or he then works magic from that basis. For it is a path of entry into the Pagan realms of deep enchantment.

The word 'pray' can be defined as the action of making a devout supplication to God, or an object of worship, to beseech earnestly or to summon to one's support. 'Prayer' can be defined as a solemn request to God, or an object of worship or an entreaty to a person.

This makes it sound as if all prayer is about saying 'Can I have' or 'I want' or 'Give me'. Even within the terms of a conventional or mainstream view of prayer, this is obviously too narrow a definition. For while most prayers are motivated by, and built around, a request for a healing or beneficial change, there are other strands. To begin with, there is an invocation of a deity, with a view to achieving a sense of communion (a healing and magical experience, in itself). There may be a celebration of a deity: that is, a joyful response, a sort of 'inner singing'. Again, this in itself is magical. There may be a thanksgiving, a grace. Or a verbal offering: that is, a spiritual vow. Blessings may even be conferred upon others, in the deity's name. Almost all prayers contain more than one of these diverse themes. Magical prayers always do.

Having said this, the prayer that is probably most usual of all among human beings, is a supplication, a beseeching: 'HELP. If you're there, show me what to do. Help me survive this!' I would bet that, worldwide, this is the most common prayer, sadly.

So how do the more varied prayers of the wildwood mystic develop? One description of Pagan prayer came to me from one of my familiars, a British 'cunning man' (a village wiseman), who was last incarnate in the ninth century. What follows is a transcript of the dialogue I had with him, using a type of automatic writing (which is to say, writing which is directed by a spirit presence – a written mediumship).

'Did you pray much when you were alive?' I asked him.

'Surely, there is not a cunning man who does not pray?' was his shocked reply.

'Did you have any special, particular prayers to say?'

'There is one that I say but it is secret. It is the heart of my power to bring healing.'

'Who taught it to you?'

'The spirits. I found it with their help. My sister found hers beneath a wind that was like a long, light blanket. But mine was underneath water.'

'How do you mean, it was under the water?'

'I swam and was under a long time, without breath, until it came to me, from the water spirits.'

'Can you tell it to me?'

'No, I have said it is secret. There are prayers to be said aloud and shared, and prayers to be held in silence.'

'How can the prayers that are most healing be found by today's wisewoman and cunning men?'

'First, you must know the reality of death. You must feel in your spirit your own body's mortality. That is what must be. But that is not all it takes. You must open your spirit to the prayers that are being said by all created things. Then let one claim you. With a light heart, you must be prepared to be possessed by the prayer.'

'Possessed? That's a word most people find frightening. What does it mean, to be possessed by a prayer?'

'To let the prayer take command of your destiny.'

'How would we know if it was the right prayer, or not?'

'By its effect. By whether or not you could heal and bless with power. By the charms and songs you made, having said it. By whether or not your life had good purpose.'

'To whom should we pray?'

'To the powers of creation in all, from the star spaces to the worm belly. To the spirit of recovery from ill. To the spirit that brings wisdom through time. To these, or any other faces of what is good. To the Lady. Or to the Lord.'

'Why should a prayer be secret?'

'Most prayers are not. Most are to be shared. Hillsides are good places to pluck out prayers that are meant to be anyone's to say. These can be said alone, or with many others. The spirits will tell you if a prayer is just for you to know, secretly.'

The cunning man went on to say that not all prayers have words – they can be enacted. A prayer can be a movement, a dance, the making of a picture, the placing of flowers in a room, some music, a herb potion.

Secret prayers – like Rumpelstiltskin's name, or like certain Eastern mantras – depend for their power upon being told to nobody else. Secrecy remains an acknowledged aspect of modern witchcraft (in spite of the many books, like my own previously published ones, that have shared witches' practices with the world). For there is an old tradition that when you have cast a spell, you should never speak of it to anyone – except, perhaps, to another witch. And amongst witches, there is the dictum that we must be able 'to know, to will, to dare and to keep silent'. You must know how to cast a spell, be determined to achieve your goal, have the courage to undertake the magic and, just as importantly, refuse to speak about it. The roots of a spell must always be concealed, like the roots of a plant, or nothing can grow. A magical prayer must be hidden, too. Or, at least, the one which is the heart of your power must be hidden. The cunning man's secret prayer seems to be connected with these themes, and perhaps with the wish not to dissipate the power of his innermost spiritual commitment (the prayer he is 'possessed by') by exposing it to everyone's comments. Certain aspects of prayer have been, and remain, a private matter. However, the cunning man would always share in community prayer, or group ritual.

For today's wildwood mystic, these distinctions still seem to be valid. However, since we are not practicing a mainstream religion, our prayers are more likely to remain private, for the most part. In any case, wildwood mysticism, like hedge witchcraft, is mainly a solitary pursuit.

Likewise, the finding of the one secret prayer that is the heart of an increased magical power, is a solitary matter. It consists of being open to 'the prayers that are being said by all created things': being able to hear what trees, rocks and hills might pray; knowing what prayers a hawk or badger or wren might say. In other words, to let nature spirits be our guides. This was the cunning man's way, as he described it. The present day wildwood mystic may find his or her own most heartfelt prayer in some other manner. One thing is certain: it is not revealed to any of us until we are ready. Such prayers do not come immediately upon this path, but as a culmination of years of faithful exploration and experimentation.

The concept of the personal secret prayer is not, so far as I know, a recognized Pagan tradition. I only know of it myself because of the cunning man's guidance, received psychically – but it is worth considering, if only because the search may be as worthwhile and interesting as the finding. Simply by keeping this quest in mind, we may make many magical discoveries and gain much mystical insight. At any time that you may have found such a prayer, then record it, say it regularly and study it's meaning. It is able, spiritually, to set the tone of your whole life. It could change your destiny, because your spirit and soul and mind, and then circumstances, will be colored by it (or so the Cunning Man tells me). A tantalizing and exciting idea!

Within this book, I will explain how to design any hedge witch's prayer, whether secret or shared openly. By sharing many of my own prayers, I hope to teach by example. The prayers in this book are all effective, in spite of being made public, but also I shall explain how to create fresh prayers, with the help of a familiar spirit. I shall unravel the technical aspect of prayers and their construction. However, you do not always have to write your own new prayers. It is fine to use any in this book, if they feel right to you, since all are based on traditional ideas. In any case, they may make a good starting point if you are new to wildwood mysticism and hedge witchcraft.

There is no hierarchy of prayer. The secret prayer is not better than the public or shared one, nor a new one necessarily better than one that has been tried and tested (or vice versa). They simply serve different functions.

Superstition has always surrounded the entire subject of prayer. For instance, the *Egyptian Book of the Dead* conveys the idea that repetition of certain prayers could ensure the favor of the Gods in the afterlife. Roman Catholics have tended to believe in a very similar theory: that the recitation of 'Our Father' and 'Hail Mary' a prescribed number of times is enough to get you back in God's good books, after a wrongdoing. This is, of course, ridiculous. It is obviously changed behavior that counts, not a mindless chanting of certain words, like a schoolchild doing 'lines'.

However, the repetition of prayers can have a part to play, for the genuine mystic. This is because it is rhythmic and semihypnotic and so can induce a light trance state, in which we may achieve communion with realms of spirit. Rhythmic chanting of a prayer can lull the everyday mind into quietness, in which a dreamier, more psychic state of mind can arise. Many witches use the chanting of Goddess names for this purpose – the prayer of invocation as a mantra.

But whatever kind of prayer we say, and whether repeated or not, to pray is to address mystery. For the wildwood mystic, this means to psychically enter the realm of the world tree.

4   Behind Hedge Magic

If this is to be a book of magical prayers for the hedge witch – who is, first and foremost, a wildwood mystic – then we must define what these terms mean. First, what is a hedge witch? Is she or he to do with plants, especially? Or to do with what grows in those thin strips of woodland that divide one field from another in Britain? When I first wrote the book *The Wiccan Path* (known in Britain as *Hedge Witch*) I found that many people were asking me whether I was a herbalist. They assumed that hedge witchcraft must be about using, medicinally, the many wild plants that grow in hedge banks and amongst the hedge trees – a reasonable assumption, considering that village wisewomen and cunning men of the past would have done just that. But nowadays, this is not so. For while some hedge witches are medical herbalists, most are not. The term simply means 'solitary witch'. I derived it from the nineteenth century term 'hedge priest'. This meant a priest who belonged to no church or group, but simply went his own way, teaching or ministering beside the hedgerow, informally. 'Hedge school', another nineteenth century term, had the same connotations. It meant an informal school – simply a group of villagers, educating themselves. Thus, hedge witch: a solitary witch, answerable to no one, belonging to no coven; claiming the right to be what she or he was born to be – magical; learning alone from familiar spirits or by trial and error, or from other witches, informally; not governed by a large movement or institution but, nonetheless, authentic; a natural, however unrecognized; a born witch. However, I'd like to point out here that many witches who work in covens are also 'born witches', and that most do work alone, sometimes. There is not always a hard and fast division between the coven witch and hedge witch, but the term is applied, normally, to those who always work alone.

The term has caught on. It is now widely used, here in Britain, to mean any lone witch, a solitary spellcaster. The use of plants – for their magical resonance and symbolism – may feature in many of our spells, but most of us do not have the medical knowledge of herbs as a treatment for illnesses that our foremothers and fathers would have had. So we leave that to the trained practitioners, qualified herbalists and the like, and concentrate on our magic. We use skills like ritual, visualization and enchantment (the magical use of words).

Some other terms used nowadays, which mean much the same as hedge witch, are wisewoman, wild witch, cunning man, lone witch or village witch. These all denote a solitary practitioner of magic.

What makes a hedge witch authentic? First, an ability to sense the spirit in all things. Not necessarily to see or hear nature spirits, or not at first, but simply to feel that they are there, along with a strong sense of all psychic atmospheres. Second, a natural feeling for ritual action. The inclination to mentally dedicate something (like letter writing or planting seeds or making a display of moss and feathers and pebbles, for example) to the reweaving of fate, a spellcasting. The authentic hedge witch can feel the effect psychically, because they have a fey spirit. And so they live in more than one dimension: within the mortal world, yet with an awareness of psychic energy fields and the links between these and life.

Such knowledge does not come all at once, but in a born witch there are always glimmerings, from childhood onward.

For a born or hedge witch, there is a connection between our activities – arts and crafts, gardening, walking, love, child-care, work and so on – and magic. When simple things are consecrated, by prayer and magical intention, they are imbued with the power of ritual and become spells – as when a woman who is sewing a quilt begins to picture the peaceful sleep of those who will lie under it. The sewing becomes a spell, as she weaves the thread of fate for those sleepers, and asks the Goddess to bless her work. Or, for example, when a man, hanging a picture of trees in his living room, then visualizes the leaf-filtered light of woods, and woodland atmosphere, spreading throughout his home. He dedicates it as a wild place of healing magic, and asks that the spell be blessed.

Hedge witchcraft can be this immediate. It is not dependent on much equipment or ritual regalia. It is more about consecration of what we are doing. However, it does have an area of some formality, centered on prayer and the tending of an altar, to make sure we do keep the thread of our magical existence, by having some structure. We learn from folk tradition and the books of other witches and inner guidance, to reinterpret witchcraft for today. Our ancestors used magic all the time: blessing spells for the home, to make the fire stay lit overnight, or for good health, or love, or an increase in the birth of lambs or cattle, or even to help butter form while churning the milk! The famous Carmina Gadelica, a nineteenth century collection of Celtic poems, shows how naturally, and with how much lyricism, our foremothers and fathers used the practice of enchantment. This was the skill once common to all native cultures, all over Europe, or so we may safely assume. It springs from a knowledge that we are all part of one biosphere, psychically, as well as physically, interconnected with plants and animals and all the elements. This is an awareness possessed by all those who live close to the earth.

Today's Pagan returns to our ancestors' feeling for the
connectedness of all beings in one Earth dance, and for each
creature and tree and pool's separate spirit – but with a new

knowledge; the terrible knowledge of what it feels like to live in a world where the vibrant spirits of places and plants and creatures are now discounted, as though nonexistent. For the world says that nature is empty, that it's just raw materials to be exploited for our needs. In contrast, the witch speaks with the spirits of nature, or even speaks as these same spirits:

To be a witch. One who speaks for the tree roots and stones. Who speaks with the tree roots' and stones' voices. One who speaks as the grass and rivers. Who speaks as fields and woods and hills and valleys and the salt marshes and waves and tides. Yet who speaks as what is close to home. With the mouse's voice or the seagull's or the fox's or badger's. One who speaks in cadences that go beyond the darkness and beyond stars, encompassing what is unmeasurable. One whose entire being vibrates to the spirits' words in nature, like a reed at dawn in a pool where trout swim.

That at least is the aspiration, as told to me by my familiar spirit. Culturally, and environmentally, this is what the world needs: voices proclaiming the poetry and sacredness of the natural world, and so invoking a healing of the wasteland which humans have created; the voices of Pagan spellcasters; the witches' voices, in strength and beauty.

The witch is not someone without life problems. To love nature and magic and try to acknowledge the spirit in all creatures, in today's harsh world, is often to feel overwhelmed. In other words, being that psychically sensitive can mean that even a walk down an ordinary city street can be deeply distressing, owing to the waves of misery, despair or extreme stress coming from so many passers by. We are not all powerful. We cannot fix everything. There is only so much that we can, magically, attend to, and so we often suffer from nervous exhaustion and need to use our magic to heal ourselves. In spite of these problems, a witch stands her or his ground.

Hedge witchcraft could seem as though it hasn't got a prayer, as they say, when it comes to confronting real problems. How can lighting a candle and putting, say, a bunch of daffodils on a table and saying a short magical prayer make a serious difference in life? But such simple witchcraft can have a deep mystical power, if it is sincere: the old lady who places a vase full of loosestrife or vervain in her room, with a prayer to the Goddess for reconciliation (on the occasion of a reunion with an estranged brother or sister) is using hedge witchcraft; the single parent who buys organic potatoes, with a prayer that organic farming may increase, and the children may therefore have a better chance, is using hedge witchcraft; the man who carries an acorn in his pocket, with a prayer to the Horned God to make him both virile and protective, is using hedge witchcraft.

Each of the above examples does involve the use of a plant, in a talismanic manner, but hedge witchcraft may also be done with shells or feathers, bought or found objects, activities, song or dance. What matters is that they should form a poetic, symbolic link with the theme of the spell, and thus invoke the relevant spirit powers.

The practice that is behind hedge witchcraft, that makes it profound and powerful, is wildwood mysticism. Or, to put it another way, hedge witchcraft is wildwood mysticism in action.

A mystic can be defined as 'one who seeks by contemplation and selfsurrender to obtain union with or absorption into the deity, or who believes in spiritual apprehension of truths beyond the understanding'.

A wildwood mystic is one who approaches these goals

through worship of the Pagan deities of the three realms of the world tree. The self that we seek to surrender is the false self: the self conditioned to be out of touch with psychic and natural realities; the self taught to dismiss all intuition as silly and irrational, and all need to take account of nature's rhythms as old-fashioned, primitive and opposed to progress; the self that sees all sense of communing with nature spirits as dangerous. We seek to surrender this self, so that we may be at one with the Goddesses and Gods, and with all life.

The spiritual truths we seek which are 'beyond the understanding' are those of magical tides and the mysteries of life, death and rebirth.

There are five key practices for wildwood mystics.

1 Pagan prayer
2 Journeys to wild and sacred places (pilgrimage)
3 Pagan ritual
4 Inner journeying (trancework and visualization)
5 Living a dedicated life (honoring nature, environmentally)

The practice around which all the others revolve is the first one – prayer. For instance, a physical journey to a stone circle or other sacred place is made into a pilgrimage most easily by our prayers. If, on arrival, we pray to the spirit of the place, and to the Great Goddess and God, then the veils part. That is, the psychic and magical aspects of the area are no longer concealed from us. We can then gain realizations and work magic.

Similarly, with our inner journeying, we can gain admission to the right level or domain within inner realms by praying to Pagan deities for guidance.

Prayer is also the foundation of Pagan ritual, and for the living of a life of ritual meaning – a consecrated life.

Each of these practices embodies an aspect of what is

behind and within hedge witchcraft, empowering it. Spells give a wildwood mystic's path direction and purpose, for what use is mysticism if it does not serve life?

Many of the following chapters will give prayers and spells for down-to-earth subjects: fulfillment in love, good fortune, prosperity, good health and a secure home and so on. In contrast to mainstream conceptions of mysticism, that of the wildwood does not seek to separate us from life or other people. It does not encourage us to transcend nature or deny natural instincts. Instead, it aims at a balanced fulfillment for all – a fullness of life.

5 Initiation in the Wildwood Mysteries

Wildwood mysticism does not mean only the mystical experiences we may have in connection with trees. It is about rivers and streams and seas and faerie presences, all nature spirits of plants and beasts and also communion with the Sun, Moon and stars, and even far constellations. It is the mysticism of all that is natural and Pagan, of all that exists around the symbolic world tree. However, if you want initiation upon the path of the wildwood mysteries – the spirituality of the solitary witch – it is best to begin with a pilgrimage to a tree. Choose one that seems, to you, especially magical. It might be an oak, or a silver birch, or an apple or ash tree, as each of these was revered as a living example of the world tree by European ancestors. If you do not live in Europe, or are not of European descent, then there may be some other type of tree that feels more appropriate to you. However, in the end, the species of tree does not matter half as much as the fact that it is a tree. Any tree will do, to symbolize the connection between the three realms – and the unity of life. Any tree can resonate, for you, with nature spirits and underground streams and rivers and stars between branches.

Choose the wildest place that you know of, for your pilgrimage. If you live in a large city, this may not be easy. You might have to look on Ordnance Survey maps to find an area of woodland outside (or even within) the city boundary. Or can you remember some place you visited as a child and it seemed enchanted? You might go there again, or perhaps return to an old orchard that you know, somewhere. Finally, though, if you have restrictions on your mobility and live somewhere far from the country, you may have to settle for a tree in your own or a friend's garden, or in a park. This may not seem much of a pilgrimage, but if you are sincere and are able to spend time alone, uninterrupted, beside the tree, to say your initiation prayer, then this will do.

Great forests once covered most of our island, and any garden tree – elder, apple, hawthorn or holly, whatever you have – can still evoke the wildwood that existed for us, as a phantom presence. Trees in parks can be large and long established. Many were there before the park was created, when the place was still fields and woods. Consider the following:

The God Odin is said to have hung upside down for nine days, upon an ash tree, in order to learn the magic of the Triple Goddess of Fate, who dwelt beside a spring underneath the tree. She gave him the secret of the runes, which he brought back to aid suffering humanity. For the runes could be used to weave healing spells, as well as to foretell the future.

The Goddess Nimue used enchantment to create a tower out of hawthorn, as a magical retreat for the prophet Merlin, who is the guardian of Britain's inner treasures – that is, of the magical resonances found within the land.

The Faerie Queen (another way of naming the Goddess of the Underworld) traditionally gives to poets an apple, as she did to Thomas the Rhymer. This confers upon them the powers of bardic utterance and prophecy.

The Goddess Brigid, the poet, healer and craftswoman, is especially associated with rowan trees.

The oak is known, traditionally, as 'doorkeeper to the mysteries', meaning those of the spirit realms and also of all plant magic.

These are just some of the themes that may be evoked by a wildwood initiation. You are attempting communion with deities and spirits of the above kind. You may therefore become a weaver of unusually powerful word spells, or a seer or healer. More humbly, you may be asked to 'tend woodland altars' by looking after some plants or animals. Who knows? At any rate, your life will change, gradually but for good, if you stay upon this path. And the changes may be unexpected.

At the time of a new moon (or within a few days after that) go to the tree you have chosen and sit under it quietly, and alone. So as not to be interrupted or distracted, you may have to choose an unpopular time for this, like early in the morning, to get the place to yourself. But if you are a woman, and feel vulnerable alone in the country, or in a park at dawn, then you might like to take a friend to sit not too far away, and watch over you.

Sit quietly, with your eyes closed. Visualize the insects and creatures that may fly or crawl or run round the trunk: butterflies, beetles, flies and bees, mice and voles, perhaps toads, slow-worms or even, very late at night, the occasional fox. And then there are the birds that nest in the branches, or fly past. All these are the representatives of the whole living world. Picture, too, wildflowers, mosses, ferns or grass. If you start to picture other creatures from more watery environments, or from a far-off land, then this is good. You are, after all, sitting beside an example of the world tree. You might like to picture some people around it, or even mythical creatures. But you should begin with the wildlife that is local.

Next, visualize the tree roots going down into the earth,

perhaps going down as far below as the branches grow high above (this is said to be the case with oak trees). Picture them reaching between cracks in the rock underneath the soil, snaking their way down to underground caverns. Wherever you are, park or garden or wild forest, the roots go down to the caves below. Down to the underworld. Imagine this cavern stops being dark, grows dim as twilight, and then bright and brighter. You are seeing with underworld eyes. Perhaps there is a small pool or lake, with a glass-bottomed boat on it. In the middle of the lake is a green faerie island, with a green mound or hill there, a faerie tor. The island is huge. It looked quite tiny, when you first noticed it, but it contains a whole realm of elves of many kinds and of creatures, trees, places. Fish are in the waters around the island. Four streams leave the lake – one going east, one south, one west and one north, each taking the waters of renewal to the world.

Finally, visualize the branches above you. Between them, see the sky. The Sun is up there, radiating warmth, light, life and healing. A golden gift, all day. Illumination, even when it rains. The Moon is there, also (for at new moon, she is above us in the sky, along with the Sun). Feel her strong magnetic pull, upon the tides of fate, the seas, our feelings. The Moon's light rules our inner and dream worlds, bestowing visions. (No wonder witches revere the Moon.) Now the light fades, the night sky appears high above you. Picture the stars, the constellations. They are glowing with mystery and power. They speak of infinity, the untold reaches of space, its immensity.

Next, try to picture or sense the three realms at once. The sky above us, between branches, all creatures round the trunk, the faerie realm below and within. See how the tree links them, how powers from each may affect the whole tree. How there is just unity.

When you are ready, say something like this:

I am one with all creatures around the world tree.
I serve the Goddess and God of wildwood mysteries.
Pagan and untamed, may I become wise and free.

Now say the following prayer, (which it is better to have memorized, but you may read it) or say your own version of something like it. Wildwood mysticism is meant to be wild – that is, it is your spirituality, which no one can foist on you, or tell you how to do. This book is supposed to point the way, with suggestions. It is not a final version, as if there ever could be one! Unlike the conventional faiths, Paganism does not have a holy book or a fixed liturgy – just the one we are all writing continually, in our own spirits, changing and amending it as we learn. So say what you want to say. Add to this prayer if you want to do so, or leave out any line which does not feel right.

Prayer for Initiation as a Wildwood Mystic

Great Lady and Lord of all creation, I call upon you.
Goddess and God of the three realms around the
world tree, I ask you to hear me. Grant me an entry
to Pagan realms of mysticism. Let my spirit enter. I
ask your blessing and protection and I seek wisdom.
Let me find friends among the denizens of the bright
faerie realms and nature spirits, and among the
winged presences that bestow exaltation. I seek to
learn from them about your truth. I seek assistance
from them, that I might serve life. Great Goddess and
God, I turn to you. May I become wise and free, upon
the wildwood path. So may it be.

Bury a lock of your hair within the earth, beside the tree trunk.
Pause, with your eyes closed, and see what you feel, what you experience. Notice any feelings in your body or any

sense of spirit presences. You may not feel anything dramatic right away. Becoming aware of the spirits of nature, or of the faerie realm and the powers and energy fields from stars, planets or luminaries, is a gradual process. You may not meet with the elves just yet (though if you stay upon the path, you will in the end). Magical prayer is a gentle method, so normally, there is a slow awakening over years. It is both thorough and safe. However, you may be surprised by what you do now experience. It should be subtle but quite unmistakable. A sense of meaning, an awareness.

Close with a prayer for your soul's protection, as it is not wise to return to everyday life in a state of too much psychic openness. The flood of impressions from television and radio, other people's thoughts and words, and psychic resonances in the atmosphere, can be too much for anyone recently sensitive to very subtle impressions. Say something like this:

In the names of the Goddess and God, I now cast around me the aura of protection. May the guardian spirits who attend upon all wildwood mystics watch over and guide me. And may no ill will come near me, but let me walk always in love and wisdom.

Picture yourself surrounded by a sphere of blue light, a protective aura like that around Mother Earth. Always end any mystical experience, magical prayer session or any work of spellcasting, with some word magic for protection, and the casting of a blue aura around yourself.

To help you along the wildwood path, the following studies can be undertaken.

1   To honor the Goddess and God of the underworld, learn of the roots of things. Read about psychology and mythology, for these show archetypal patterns that underlie all our lives. Faerie tales are our Northern European myths. So is the matter concerning King Arthur and the Grail, especially the older, pre-Christian versions. If you do not feel like studying these things in scholarly depth, that is fine. It is far better to read a few books, or even a few tales, that appeal to you and hold your interest, than wade through whole boring libraries.

Try to remember your dreams. Perhaps keep a dream journal. Practice trying to see underneath. That is, to discern the real issues, in dreams or any situation.

What is profound? What is most meaningful? What are deep matters and what are superficial? Meditate on these themes.

2   To honor the Goddess and God of middle Earth, study the natural world and her creatures. What is the wildlife in your area? Do badgers live in your town? Are there hedge-hogs and foxes? If you live in the country, are there many birds? Bats? Hares? What about wild native trees? Or wild-flowers? Are you able to recognize them and to name them? Find out what the issues are for wildlife, in respect to conser-vation, near to where you live. In cities, there are often surprisingly large amounts of wild plants and wild animals – along canal and river banks, railway embankments, and in people's gardens. For instance, in our garden, we have frogs and toads, bank voles, butterflies, slugs and snails and a large variety of wild birds, which we feed regularly. Our garden, in a city suburb, is only about twelve feet by twenty-five, yet all this goes on in it.

It is also important to get to know any ancient, magical sites in your area. Where are the holy wells? Guide books or local knowledge can often tell us where the wells known for healing, or the wishing wells, might be. These are the ones that were held sacred by Pagan ancestors, and known for the fact that the waters held more than just minerals, but were a potion that affected the spirit. Long before such wells or springs were given Christian saints' names, they were revered and visited.

Similarly, do you have local hills associated with folklore? Or stone circles or any long barrows? Any such sites as these are good to visit, as a pilgrim in search of communion with the spirits of the place, and with Pagan deities. They are also ideal places for working magic. The only rule when you go there is not to leave evidence that you have been. In other words, obviously, do not leave litter. But also, do not leave offerings or other traces of ritual activity that are not biodegradable.

3   To honor the Goddess and God of the upperworld, think about what we aspire to, as a species. Is it good enough? Do you agree with most people's aims? What about your own highest aspirations? Your best ideals?

Physically, do you think we are alone in the cosmos, the only inhabited planet? If there are, or have been, others, what might they be like, or have been like, at their best? There are a lot of theories about some of our own ancestors coming from other worlds that revolved around stars other than our own Sun – interesting material to read and think about. Have you seen crop circles? Been in one? What do you think of them? Hoax or not?

Above all, can we conceive of other beings, from other more highly developed worlds, who might be more spiritually and morally evolved than we are? Whether or not they have literally existed is not the issue here. 'Real' or not, they can serve as role models, in order to help us define what we think 'right living' might be like. So what are their values? Do they preach about sin and punishment? Do they have compassion and wisdom? Would they eliminate a wrongdoer or heal and transform them?

Imagine the most wise, creative, adventurous, passionate and loving race that could exist. Write about them, paint or draw them, dream of them. They might be untamable. What a vision to help us!

Remember, also, that although we would normally associate Mother Earth with middle Earth, she can also be seen as an upper world Goddess, in the sense that she can exemplify astounding beauty and creativity, resourcefulness and a rich natural wisdom. She has our highest ideals within her, and is an example to us all. The point of looking to the stars and other planets is not to transcend her, but to attune to a level of idealism and a cosmic perspective.

Pursuing the study of the three realms is a lifelong commitment for wildwood mystics. It leads to many magical adventures and realizations. It underpins and empowers any spells that we want to do, as hedge witches. Also, the desire to practice enchantment gives a purpose to mysticism. It gives frequent and sometimes quite pressing reasons to visit a sacred site, or to enter, by Pagan prayer, the realms of spirit. This means that we have momentum upon the path, for there are always reasons in life to cast constructive spells: we may want to heal ourselves or each other, or wild creatures; we may wish to invoke for good fortune, or for safe travel for our friends or children; for lasting love; for new inspiration and so on. Each time, we must fly between the realms, as though on our broomsticks or winged stags or horses, to seek the help and guidance of spirits, under the protection of Pagan deities. We do this by means of the consciousness-altering power of magical prayers.

For those who wonder if such beliefs are really an authentic European tradition, it might help to consider the following passages.

Underworld spirituality, concerned with fate-spinning faeries from hollow hills, long barrows and sacred islands, is clearly indigenous, as explained by W.Y. Evans-Wentz, in *The Fairy Faith in Celtic Countries* written in 1911.

Reverence for the magical, mystical properties of plants and the wisdom of animals – the spirituality of middle Earth – is obvious in our folklore, and in beliefs descended to us from our forebears, concerning healing and spellcraft.

Belief in the importance of Moon, Sun, and stars is very strongly displayed by stone circles. Our ancestors built them to align with the sunrise (or set) at the solstices, or with the

Moon's nineteen-year cycle in relation to the stars. Some of them are also orientated toward stars or constellations.

The idea of the world tree, that links the three levels, seems to have been worldwide and was certainly prevalent in Europe.

6 A Consecration of the Wildwood Altar

By now, it will be clear that you need an altar, at which you can pray and work magic regularly. Witches say magical prayers anywhere, wherever they are. Spells can be cast at the bus stop, or in the town park, in an emergency. Or you may be working your magic while sewing, digging in the garden, carving a piece of wood, or baking a cake. For maximum formality, you may want to cast a full magic circle, to celebrate a special occasion, like a sabbat. This process is described at length in my book *The Wiccan Path*, and in many other books by present-day Pagans. Casting a circle and working within it is a very powerful thing to do. Any witch should know how to do this. However, as a wildwood mystic, you do not have to cast a circle for a sabbat, or any other occasion. Indeed, in a later chapter, I will explain how to celebrate the sabbats (eight seasonal festivals of the year) more informally. But the point here is that, whereas a witch might – or might not – work formally for a special purpose, an altar can be used every day, very easily, in order to give continuity in prayer and magic. It expresses your spirituality, in all its phases. By placing objects upon it, for religious purposes, you help to awaken your spirit to communion with Pagan deities. The definition of the word 'altar' is 'place for offerings to the deity'. By having a place set apart to say magical prayers, you make it possible to keep the thread, to stay true to the path of the wildwood mystic – even when you are under a great deal of pressure in life (for instance, a family crisis or work problems).

Naturally, the wildwood mystic's prayers are often said at the sacred sites, e.g. stone circles, holy wells, hills, sacred springs or long barrows; in caves or woods, or at the seashore; at such special places of beauty and power, our magical prayers are appropriate. However, if we are to be wildwood mystics in the midst of life, hedge witches even in a city, then there is a need for an altar indoors, at which we can work each day, and on which we can place things, like stones, feathers, fossils, shells and leaves, collected for magic purposes.

Having an altar means you have a small sacred site, within your own home. Not, of course, upon a ley line (unless you are very lucky!), but a place that has been consecrated and so is made sacred. How you do this is by ritually dedicating your altar to the Goddess and God, decorating it with objects that have inner and symbolic meaning, and then tending it (i.e. lighting the candles and praying there, regularly). The strength that is gained by the witch, from these daily communings, is really important to emotional and psychic survival, in what is, for many of us, a very unmagical everyday world.

It is, of course, more exciting to invoke the Pagan Goddess or God at an ancient long barrow, or on the beach at dawn, but let's face it, most of us would only go to such places on special occasions, as a pilgrimage. We do not live in them. For everyday purposes, the altar is a small, newly made sacred site, that is not at the other end of a long car or bus ride. Even if you live in the country, your indoor altar is still necessary. It is reachable in any weather and at any time of day or night. The more often deities are invoked there, familiar spirits conferred with, and magical work done, the more it begins to radiate a clear, magical energy. A forcefield is set up, in and around the wildwood altar – a psychic forcefield – which means, after a while, you may only have to stand there with your eyes closed, to attain magical consciousness or to see visions. I can vouch for this, as it has often happened to me, and I know it works for others, too.

Also, by the making of altars to Pagan deities, the wild-wood psychic dimension is brought back to our towns and cities. In other words, all the vibrance of nature's mysteries can be invoked in an urban flat, and then the whole building is healed, somewhat. The town is healed, even if just a little. For the altar becomes a wellspring of healing, due to its connection with nature spirits.

At first, you may find that attempting to pray at a table, in the corner of the bedroom or living room, defeats you. It feels mundane. What spirit presences? What psychic force-field? But if you do a rite of consecration for your altar, and continue to serve at it faithfully, real power will build up. The psychic energy that is around it will increase.

For such work, you need peace and quiet and privacy. Draw the curtains, and work by candlelight. If noise from outside or from other rooms is a distraction, then play music. This should be something instrumental and suited to the mood. Harp music can be excellent. But there are many tapes and CDs now available, meant for meditation or magi-cal work, to use as a background. Some classical music is suitable as well. Whatever you play, make sure there are no words, because otherwise, the song itself may become a distraction.

Have upon your altar two candles. You may first wish to drape whatever table or shelf you are using with a green cloth, to denote your connection with the nature and faerie spirits with whom wildwood mystics work, but have a plain wooden surface if you prefer it. As a centerpiece, between and behind the candles (that is, in the middle, toward the back) have a vase full of leafy things, greenery and branches. These could be quite small, not branches in fact, but twigs, depending upon the space that you are working in. Whatever size, they symbolize the World Tree. In winter, you can have bare twigs or evergreen leaves. The summer twigs will need to be changed quite often, as the leaves will wither, so it is best not to be too ambitious about the most magically appropriate tree for your purpose. It is more practical to use what is nearby, in your garden or a local hedgerow. If you wish to be purist, then keep a bare twig of apple, oak or ash or birch, among the greenery.

Make sure the vase holding your 'tree' is of pottery or glass or something else natural, and not of plastic. All objects upon an altar must be organic, as this honors our connection with nature, and also is said to be very much more able to resonate within the psychic dimension, the otherworld, as well as this one. A natural object, or a handmade one, could be at home within the faerie realms, and so it is suitable for the wildwood altar, meant to attract Pagan presences.

To the left, more toward the front, have a round bowl of water, in honor of the Threefold Goddess. This symbolizes her power to bring healing visions, her creative womb, from which all life comes, and her sacred cup, holding the waters of life, which bring renewal. Like the vase, this bowl should be of a dark colour, or else glass, or it could be of a silvery metal.

To the right, in honor of the God, have a musical instrument. This should be a penny whistle or ocarina or a simple wooden pipe. It symbolizes his magical powers, his fertility and his ability to waken us to the quest for our true selves. Whistles have been used since ancient times to 'call in the spirits' – that is, to signal magically to one's spirit helpers, requesting their assistance. Some very old whistles have been found that were made of sheep bone, in Britain and Ireland. Clay, wood, reed and horn were also used. Because of their phallic shape, whistles are linked with the God.

This kind of simply arranged altar will do to start with. In time, you will know what else you want to add to it. The altars of wildwood mystics are always being altered. The objects on them are freshened up, moved around or replaced altogether. An important magical theme may be represented for a year, and then disappear. This is because altars are not set pieces nor objects d'art, but living places of power and communion. To consecrate one, place upon it the following: a feather, a small dish of vegetable oil, a similar bowl of salt water, a stone and a flower. Then light the candles and say this:

The Prayer for Consecration of an Altar

Great Goddess and God, Lady and Lord of all living and of the spirits of the dead, I call upon you. You who are the magic in trees and stars, far galaxies, blades of grass, streams and oceans, hear my prayer. Bless now this altar, which I dedicate to you. Bless and hear all prayers which shall be said in this place. Bless the prayers of any others who join me here, and of my familiars. Bless all work of magic which shall be offered. Great Lady and Lord of the upperworld, middle Earth and underworld, I stand here as a sincere worshipper. Open the portals, that this altar become a place of communion with you and with spirit presences.

Pause. And then raise the vase full of twigs above the altar, in symbolic offering.

Now make the sign of an equal-armed cross within a circle, upon your altar, with the feather. Then do it again with a dab of the vegetable oil, and then with the water. Next, trace the outline of the symbol very lightly with your stone. And finally with the flower, or a blade of grass. This equal-armed cross in the circle is a pre-Christian symbol. To present-day Pagans, it means the Circle of Life, containing the elements of which all is made – namely, air, fire, water, earth and aether (or spirit). To consecrate something thus, by the power of all the elements, is to do it completely.

Now say, *I dedicate this altar to the Great Goddess and Great God, universal deities, whose mysteries are revealed in each realm round the world tree.*

If you have any connection with a particular named Goddess or God, for personal or for cultural reasons, or because they are of your locality, you can add, *And I dedicate it especially to ____ daughter of the Great Goddess and/or to ____ son of the Great God.*

Next, follow this with prayers in your own words, for guidance on your path as wildwood mystic, for wise development in magic and for healing of anyone you know who needs it. And close with the prayer for protection.

The consecration of the altar is now complete. You may wonder why it seems to have been dedicated to both wildwood mysticism and hedge witchcraft, and why I seem to have used the terms wildwood mystic and witch almost interchangeably. I repeat – this is because wildwood mysticism is often enacted in healing magic. In this way, it seeks to serve life. In the next chapter I will explain more about what such spellcraft might mean to a hedge witch and what is the approach to magic of a wildwood mystic. Wildwood mysticism is the spirituality of the solitary witch. Hedge witchcraft is the use to which wildwood mysticism can be put, for the benefit of ourselves, of other people in need and of the world at large.

7 Prayers for the Power of a Witch

To a wildwood mystic, hedge witchcraft is about power, but also it is about surrender to the great wisdom of the Fates. It is about our own quest for insight and increased wisdom. There is no doubt that to wield magic and to affect our own and others' destinies by doing so, is to have power. Many people fear witches because of this. Can witches rewrite fate for themselves and other people? Surely such power, if it works, if it is real, can only lead to abuse? How could any mortal be wise enough to know how to affect fate for the best? How could any of us be sure we would not use our magic selfishly, damaging others' rights and needs for our own ends? And isn't power the opposite of spirituality or mysticism, since it does not seem to seek surrender to a higher will, but is about the will of the witch? For witchcraft is end directed. In other words, witches cast spells when they want to get something. Or to prevent something. They want a result, tangible and material.

Yes, we witches do want a result. We do want to cast spells that affect the material world. In this, we are not so different from others who use symbols and psychodrama to bring change: the advertising industry, for instance. Yet the methods and orientation of the hedge witch, being based in wildwood mysticism, are not those of a ruthless, corrupt manipulation. We can be sure of this if we observe two rules.

The first one is that our spells should be founded on well-wishing. There is a law among all witches (apart from those who do deal in curses) which states that our magic must cause no harm. In fact, the witches' commandment is 'harm none'. In order to want to do no harm, we must wish all beings well, even those whom we don't really like much. We must wish for what will heal and transform all and brings all to harmony. In fact, a hedge witch's spell is always an enacted meditation upon this theme, for a specific practical purpose, in any instance.

This does not mean that we may not be angry with wrong-doers, nor seek to defend the helpless, but it does mean that we must work for the best outcome without thoughts of vengeance. For example, a perpetrator of violence needs to be healed as much as the victim does, in order to prevent future recurrence of the crime. This is because they are deeply sick in their soul. They may also need to be 'bound' – that is, to be magically prevented from successfully being violent again. All this is a far cry from dishing out curses to be avenged, which does no good but merely perpetuates the reasons why the criminal feels twisted, angry and violent.

In order that we do not set ourselves up as magical judge, jury and executioner, nor pit our lack of wisdom against the Fates, concerning any spell for prosperity, for instance, we remember that the means by which a magical result shall come to be are not up to us. We state our desire and we perform a small ritual for the result, but our business is only to invoke for the ultimate good of all affected by the spell. By this, the ultimate good, we do not only mean wellbeing, but also harmonious integration with life: learning, growth, an increase in wisdom.

To sum up this rule, any spell cast by a wildwood mystic is based upon aiming for a result that harms none and should improve life for everyone. This is achieved by leaving the manner in which the end is achieved in the hands of the spirits and deities, who are much wiser than we are, and also by entering into the magic in a spirit of general well-wishing. If, of course, such a benign attitude is not possible for the time being, because we are too angry, then the magic must be left until the rage has become less raw. Otherwise, we risk becoming a part of the problem, not the solution, and we risk causing ourselves as well as others great harm, eventually. This is because what you give out, you reap. As our ancestors knew, we are all connected to a huge web of 'light', the web of fate, that links us all. Therefore, what harms one harms everything.

To repeat, we can cast any spell at all, in a spirit of general well-wishing, but the wise do not stipulate how the spell should work out. In rhyme, it goes like this:

> *Cast the spell.*
> *Wish all life well.*
> *Let the spell be strong in harmony.*
> *Then let the Fates decide*
> *How it shall come to be.*

For the purpose of the hedge witch is to increase harmony, within her or himself, with the Earth and with all creatures.

The second rule to keep is this: the wise witch casts spells on the right tide of nature. That is, at the right Moon or Sun or Earth season, or the correct seatide. She or he does not attempt to work magic in the teeth of nature's rhythms, or not if worthy of the name 'witch'. In mainstream culture, on the other hand, we are taught that we should all aim to dominate nature rather than work with her. Thus, we may embrace the idea of a twenty-four-hour shopping day, force our tired bodies on with many stimulants, and simulate the sun with a lamp to get brown. This is wanting to have our wishes met at any price. But, in the Craft of the wise, we attempt to be in step with nature's tides, seeing these as but the outer expression of subtle forces in psychic dimensions.

So we do spells of increase (e.g. for health or wealth) when the Moon waxes or the tide flows or the Sun's light is increasing, and spells of decrease (e.g. to banish ill health or poverty) when the Moon wanes, the tide ebbs or the Sun declines.

To go against this rule is usually to cast a spell that fails, for our power comes from nature spirits and deities, from all that's primal and natural. If it should succeed by sheer force of will, against nature's rhythms (like so many human activities already described) then the long-term result may not be good. For something has been forced against the grain of the wood, against nature's wisdom.

From this, it can be seen that the practice of spellcraft brings the wildwood mystic into increasing union with nature's rhythms, and increases sensitivity to the moment. Magic is our yoga – that is, it inclines us to be more in step with the natural tides of the Earth and of our own bodies. It lets us know that we are all one, that there is unity, and that any spell ripples out, affecting one person, place and creature after another. If you change one thing then you, potentially, change everything. We are all one – plants, people, earthworms, slugs, deer, and the deities, past, present, future, all atoms and galaxies – we are all interlinked. To the wildwood mystic, this is not just an idea but what we feel, what we experience, while working magic. And here is a rhyme for it:

> *The wise do not*
> *try to float spells*
> *against the current.*
> *Nor oppose the Moon or Sun*
> *With a will of iron.*
>
> *Sense the flow.*
> *Know nature's direction.*
> *Let the spell work with that and so*
> *be at one with Creation.*

The hedge witch aims to practice magic by these rules. Otherwise, our efforts would not be the Craft of the wise, but only a variation on the games of power and domination played by much of humanity. The genuine witch seeks to be attuned, through wildwood mysticism, to ancient wisdom, to heal the world's soul somewhat, and to cast spells of strength and beauty.

You may already have taken a formal initiation into the practice of solitary witchcraft, as described in *The Wiccan Path* and elsewhere. If not, then you can use the following simple method. Choose a time of the full moon and make sure that you can be undisturbed (phone switched off and music playing). Light the candles upon your altar. Burn incense or a suitable essential oil. Good oils are juniper and pine for cleansing and power, and bay, yarrow or camomile for increased psychism. Good herbs to burn would be dried vervain, ash, willow, nettle or yarrow, juniper, pine or camomile (or put the flowers or leaves on your altar, together with an apple). Say the following, or something like it, which is addressed to the Great Goddess and God of all three realms.

Prayer for Initiation as a Witch

Great Lady and Lord of all changes wrought by a deep magic, you who bring the butterfly out of the chrysalis, visions from the dark night and conscious life from mud and starlight, I call upon you to make of me your priestess/priest. Open for me the paths from wildwood mysteries to service of life. Make of me a wise witch. Change me, that the power to bring beneficial change be mine. Make of me a wise witch. I give myself, give my eternal being, to becoming wisely skilled in weaving fate. So let all the work done at this altar, and elsewhere, bring healing. Make of me a wise witch.

Dip your forefinger in the bowl of water upon your altar, which is sacred to the Goddess. Inscribe an equal-armed cross within a circle on your brow. Say,

Now I am reborn as a witch priestess/priest,
by the power of the Triple Goddess of the Circle

of Rebirth, the Goddess of upperworld, underworld and of middle Earth. So may it be.

Take the whistle from your altar and say,

In the name of the God of the Wild Hunt, Wildwood and the Underworld, whom I ask to bless and to quicken my new self, I call on guardian spirits of the elements of all life. Hear me, you spirits of air, fire, water, earth and aether, and witness that I am now a witch priestess/priest. May you surround and assist me, from now on, at need. So may it be.

Play a long note on the whistle. Hear it reverberate in inner realms, calling to the spirits.

Stand silently before the altar for a while, and see what you sense happening to your body and soul in subtle ways. You may see a vision or feel a sort of trembling, as your whole being is rebalanced. Or you may seem to enter a darkness, a mystery, or feel your senses are keener, your hearing more acute. If you do not feel anything at first, lie down upon the floor with your eyes closed and wait. Meanwhile, meditate upon what a witch is and does. Do this by describing the ideal witch, within your mind. Eventually, you will know that you have been accepted. You will feel at peace.

Stand and give thanks to the Deities and spirits. Then say the prayer for protection and put out the candles.

While the Moon wanes, every night, say the following (or a variation upon it):

Prayer to the Witch Goddess for Inspiration

Great Mother of Moon, Earth and Water, Wise Goddess, you who are the power to shift shape eter-

nally, through all the myriad forms of life, you who are the journey all undertake to tell the story, uplift my spirit as a gull in flight, as the Moon's white radiance, as the hills' exhilarating height. Bless me with the meaning that cannot be explained, but is, and is transcendent. And let me live passion, mystery, purpose.

It may seem strange to pray for an increase in inspiration upon a waning Moon. However, the aim is not so much to manifest something, grow something in the world, but to turn inward, to the meaning that is concealed in darkness.

Then say this:

Prayer to the Witch God for Integrity

Wild God of all creatures, you who protect all the balance within nature, you who are the guardian of all free-spirited beings, you whom I call upon as the presence in the forest, the mystery, grant to me that I may be aligned with what remains uncorrupted. Grant to me that I may live by the principles of those who took to the forest, to make a stand for real justice, in the old stories. And with all untamed ones, may I serve the cause of life as a witch priestess/priest. Banish all within me that is not of your laws nor of an active peace.

At the New Moon, or within a few days of it, say this prayer or something like it.

Prayer for a Witch's Strength and Wisdom

Lady of the Moon upon sea and on woodland spring water, increase in me the clear potency of a witch priestess/priest, that power of waking dream that can change destiny. You who can move tides of fate by your great magnetism, who can plait the waters of life in a swift heaving flourish, all silvered with fish-scale light, grant to me your ancient gift. Strengthen my magic, the Moon in me, that I may cast spells of healing and blessing, bringing a new and wild harmony and freedom. And open my eyes to path-ways that lead to wisdom. Clear my sight.

Then say this, or a variation upon it:

Prayer to the Witch God for Strength and Wisdom

God of the upperworld, middle Earth and under-world, you who are the lightning flash and thunder, changing the atmosphere, the fertile stag and the faerie world's mariner, bringing us all to the other-world's distant shores, within our souls and our spirits, increase in me the bright power to bring bene-ficial change. You are the one whose magician wand or staff can open doors in the Earth, leading to faerie realms, begin new life, open our minds and hearts. Let me wield such force for good transformation, but guide me in wisdom, that all my spells be cast in love and harmony.

If you are a woman, you may wish to say only the prayer to the Goddess, upon the new moon. If you are a man, you may prefer to say the one to the God, alone. But it is fine for each sex to say both of them.

Your wildwood initiation, as a witch, is now complete.

8 Prayers and Spells for Health

A witch's spells are all meant, in the broadest sense, to bring healing or to restore harmony in some way. But in this chapter, we will look at some magical prayers and rites which may be used to heal actual diseases. Health is both simple and complex to the wildwood mystic who practices hedge witchcraft. It is simple because it means being in harmony within ourselves and with all Earth's creatures – that's all. Harmony concerning what we eat, how we sleep, what we do with our lives, where we live, whether we are creative and how we are in our relationships with other beings. It is complex because the reasons why these requirements are often not met are dependent upon the culture within which we live – whether it is rich or poor, at peace or at war, environmentally caring or greedy, just to everybody or elitist etc. – as well as on our own psychology, genetic inheritance and strength of spirit.

To put this another way, none of us can expect to be fully healthy all the time, until the world is. Even we who live in wealthy countries and in beautiful places still breathe polluted air, eat and drink food and water that is tinged with pesticides, and are subject to a wide variety of economic, social and personal pressures. The only kind of person to be permanently fit in such a world would be one who lived in a bubble – and the bubble would have to have a miraculous private supply of clean air, food and water! Certainly no wildwood mystic is likely to conform to this self-serving pattern, even if it were possible. In fact, being more psychic and sensitive than most, we are more than usually open to stresses of all kinds. So, it's just as well that we can protect ourselves with a variety of healing spells, as well as (if we're lucky) spend much time in nature 'recharging our batteries'.

To reiterate: nothing will prevent us from ever getting ill at all, or not until we have helped to heal the whole world, however many lifetimes this takes us all to achieve. The good news is that our mystical efforts and rites help us and others to be more likely to recover, and much more quickly!

As a first line of approach, we may pray to the deities of middle Earth, about how we, physically, live our lives.

Prayer to the Earth Goddess for Healing

Mother Earth, grant to ____ [name them] a solid foundation for her/his/my health and whole life. I pray to you as the mother of all, the creative one who shapes and upholds existence. You are the mother of forests and oceans and all creatures, everything that lives. Help ____ [name them] to become rooted into your rhythms and in harmony with your laws of life. As though she/he/I were a tree, help her/him/me to plunge roots into your strength and be nourished, and so grow stronger, both grounded and free. Restored in health. So may she/he/I live to create beauty and realize every vision of harmony.

Prayers like the above are best said outside with your feet on the earth – barefoot, if it's warm enough. If indoors, sense the earth under the floor coverings, and visualize her strength and creativity in the form of all the grass, flowers, trees, pools and rocks, birds and beasts, crystals, hills and valleys that she makes.

This may be followed by a prayer to the God of all nature for his help and guidance.

Prayer for Healing to the Green God

Green Horned God of woodland and of wild places, I call to you – guardian of all the animals! You who guide creatures to find herbs that heal them and to know when to rest or eat and when not to, I ask you to guide ____ [name them]. Lead her/him/me to the best remedies and to healing. Whether these come via a health practitioner or by the right changes in life, may health be restored. And may your blessing be on us all. May all be led to live in ways that are best for our own health and that of all beings.

Pich up a stone, to represent mother earth, and say something like, Mother Earth, *I bless this stone in your name, as a link with your great strength and your healing magic.*

Then take a leaf or some grass to represent mother earth's partner, the Green God. Stain the stone green, saying, *Green God, your word is on all alive places. By this sign, may ____ [name the person] receive true healing.*

Give the stone to the one who is ill. It should be kept near to where they sleep – on a bedside shelf or a table. If you have done the spell for a creature or place, not for a human, the same rule still applies. Put it under the animal's bedding. Or, if it is a place that has become diseased, just take the stone there and leave it somewhere that feels suitable. Of course, the prayers may need adapting (especially for a place). In any case, these are not rigid formalities, just guidelines.

These prayers concerning how we live, and the need for physical changes or remedies, are our first resource. However, an illness may have a deep hidden cause, that is located in our psychology, or in the psychic dimension. There may be a number of unknown factors in ill health, that could range from living in an unhealthy psychic atmosphere to having creative blocks, being in unspoken conflict with a person or with a spirit, harboring grudges, being in trauma or having emotional wounds of one kind or another. These things are underworld matters. They are about subtle and possibly hidden things that detract from our fulfillment and put us at odds with fate.

The prayers to our Mother Earth and the Green God are best said in springtime or summer, but may be said anytime, as needed. Those to the underworld deities, however, are best in autumn or winter, or at any time of year when the Moon is on the wane, (or on the ebb tide, if you're by the sea).

You may pray to the Goddess and/or the God separately, or to both together, as in what follows.

Prayer to the Goddess and God of the Underworld for Healing

Lady and Lord of the hollow hills and underground pools and sea caves and all underworld places, I call upon you to send real assistance to ____ and heal her/his/my sickness. Banish all deep causes for any illness. Let these be washed away. Let any resistance to good health be transformed. Let all bad patterns within her/his/my fate that lead to disharmony be changed to good ones. Let there be a cleansing of destiny and let all bad influences upon health be gone. You, Goddess, who ordain the plot of all our lives, and you, God, who help us to understand it, guide her/him/me in a profound quest for well-being. And let her/him/me emerge into renewed health.

Now take a small piece of cloth, like a hair tie or neck scarf, belonging to the ill person. Wash it in warm, soapy water, to which you have added five drops of juniper oil, or a half cup of cider vinegar. Just before plunging the cloth in the water, say, *This cloth is the weaving in the soul of* ____ [name them] *that prevents her/him/me from being well. As I wash, so may this pattern of destiny be cleansed, removing all hindrances to well-being, of any kind. Removing all unhealthy influences, whether internal or external, from heart and mind. So may the pattern of fate from now on be one of good health for* ____ *in the names of the deities.*

When ready, give the dry cloth to the owner, all fresh and smelling of juniper (or cider vinegar) and ask them to wear it for at least one day. If you are doing this spell for an animal or place, then you can buy a small piece of cloth and link it with them by leaving it where they sleep or on site, for nine nights. After it is washed and dried, you can return it.

Sometimes, illnesses are linked with lack of spiritual energy, a feeling that your ideals have become small or narrow, that you don't look above the horizon. This feeling – that your aspirations have been badly damaged, or that you never seem uplifted, but always nose-to-the-grindstone in spiritual shabbiness or in depression – may be undermining you, physically. If so, then you need the light of the Moon or Sun or Stars, or the Moon's magnetic pull or the Sun's vibrant warmth and strength. Prayers must then be said to upper-world deities. You may know it is the Moon's mystery or the Sun's warmth and joy or the Stars' guidance that you crave. But if you're not sure, then you may need to pray to each of them. The prayers can be something like this.

Prayer to the Moon Goddess for Healing

Lady of the Moon above, giver of visions, you who are Goddess of poetry, as well as mystery, restore the meaning to the life of ____ [name them]. *Grant a renewed inspiration that leads to health. Bestow a dream or an inner sign of beauty, one that she/he/I can understand. Lady of inner sight in darkness, give healing visions and new sense of purpose.*

If the Sun's light is needed, the prayer might be this one.

Prayer to the Sun God for Healing

Great Sun God of strength and vitality, give health to ____. Grant vibrant living. Give her/him/me renewed warmth of heart. And give of spiritual illumination to us all, increasing our joy in life.

As a witch, I am happy to pray to the Moon Goddess and Sun God, as is our tradition. But many Pagans feel happier to worship a Sun Goddess and Moon God. This is just as valid, and there are many precedents for it worldwide. My own opinion is this: the Sun, Moon and stars are but physical counterparts of kinds of spiritual energy. They manifest something divine, mysterious. Of course, that energy, in every case, has both a female and male aspect. So there is both a Sun Goddess and Sun God, a Moon God and a Moon Goddess. We are not praying to lumps of rock or balls of burning gas, but to divine presences who are both or either gender. For anything may express the mother of all life and/or her son, the all father. It is a matter of preference how we see them. Either way, we will be correct, and there are traditions supporting each point of view.

Prayer to Star Deities for Healing

Great Lady and Lord of the Stars, who represent to us

guidance, I call upon you. Rekindle hope in ____, who has lost the way in the quest for health. Shine your light in her/his/my soul. Bring back a sense of faith; bring her/him/me from thoughts of death to life. Give a new beginning.

Prayers to the Sun should be said in the day and those to the Moon or stars at night. Though remember, the Moon's light is not above us in the day, but her magnetic power is, in the time from halfway to the new moon until halfway to the full.

To follow these prayers with magic, stand a glass jar or bottle of spring water in the moon, sun or starlight, for at least one hour. Then use it to anoint the ill person, place or creature. (If it is a person, you can bathe their brow with it.) Letting starlight shine on water may not be too easy, if you live in the city. It tends to be terribly obscured by streetlights. But if you take a clear glass jar full of spring water, then hold it up till you can see the stars through it, and visualize the light entering the water, this will do.

Before leaving the subject of healing, I would like to add that sickness is a part of life and not always entirely negative. It can have a part to play in allowing someone to process grief or disillusionment, or in spurring us on to seek the real causes of unease in our lives. It can give us time in which to rest and reconsider priorities. The wise witch is therefore not phobic about ill health, but able to see its place in the larger scheme. From a wildwood mystic's perspective, it teaches something each time. The whole quest for healing is linked with the way we live, who we are, on every level.

Finally, I cannot leave this chapter without including some prayers for the biggest form of healing, the one that concerns our relationship with all beings, environmentally.

Prayer to Mother Earth to Heal the Human Spirit

Our Mother Earth, Great Lady of Creation, you who have given birth to every land and all creatures and plants and to all people, we call upon you. We know that you can heal and restore the balance of nature, as you have done before. We know that after each human catastrophe, you have clothed the land again, in flowers. After each abuse, or after war, you break down poisons. Over years, you cover buildings and battlefields with plants and creatures and bring back the beauty. We ask you to change us, restore us, within our spirits. Let your wise magic make us new in harmony, that we may live in peace and creativity and in adventure, with harm to none. Bring us to wisdom.

Prayer to the Underworld Deities to Heal the Human Spirit

Great Goddess and God of the memory's storehouse and of the true source of true actions, be with us. Help us to understand ourselves and each other. Lady and Lord of the deep caverns, the underground rivers, the buried treasures, guide us to see and know and come to terms with our reasons for feeling as we do. Bring to light hidden potential for goodness, locked up in whatever gives fright. Let all that is underground, in our souls, flow out in fulfilling purpose. For it is only that which is stagnant that breeds corruption. And by you, we can become one with what moves and lives.

Prayer to the Sky Deities to Heal the Human Spirit

Great Lady and Lord of night and endless starshine, Lady and Lord of time and what is timeless, we call upon you now. Help us escape from all false limitations. We see your realm far beyond us and cannot imagine what is beyond the beyond. Break us free of that which keeps us in chains of oppression or violence or pettiness. Make our capacity for love and wisdom be limitless and based in wonder.

With imagination, many magical rites can be devised to follow such prayers as these. When rites for healing succeed, there is this:

Grace for Good Health

Thank you

Thank you

Thank you

9 Prayers and Spells for Wealth

Health, wealth and happiness are all connected; at least, you cannot be healthy, or really very happy, if too poor to buy enough food, or if suffering from stress about how to pay the rent or bills. However, wealth can be defined in many ways. It is goods, cash and property, a good income, savings. But it is also skills, talents, opportunities and the privilege of being able to live in a prosperous and fertile land. And, in a sense, it is resourcefulness, the ability to make much out of what you have – to see the possibilities and to be creative.

Most of this chapter will have to do with prayers for material prosperity, or solid cash, in a context of realization that real wealth is based in the right relationship with all nature, the land, other species. But, before going deeper into that subject, I would like to share something I've been told. Recently, I asked my familiar spirit to assist me in a rite for prosperity – which she was happy to do. Before setting to work, however, she made this pronouncement: 'Honey and iron attend you! There is a horseshoe full of honey that does not spill nor ever empty. It is the wealth you need the most!'

There are many ways I could interpret this lovely symbol of a horseshoe full of honey that does not spill, but the first thing that comes to mind is that an upright horseshoe, usually nailed onto a door or beam, is an old talisman for good luck (as well as being a protective symbol). So, is the best form of wealth the possession of good luck? And what else does the cup-shaped or lunar crescent-shaped object, magically full of sweet honey that never spills from each side, really mean? A good relationship with a marriage partner (which I do have – certainly, this is great wealth). Horseshoes are especially associated with good luck at a wedding. The symbol also reminds me of a chalice. Perhaps it resembles the mythical Grail, which heals the wasteland, restoring leaves to the withered trees and bringing new growth from the barren earth; the Grail, seen in an earthy, more homely form than that of a silver cauldron with pearls round the rim, or a crystal cup. This brings me back, in fact, to the theme that a right relationship with the land (environmentally) is the only foundation for lasting riches, for the nations and so for the people – for individuals. There is much to be said about this, but where to begin?

A tree is wealthy if it grows in good land and has rain, sunlight and clean air. It is the same, in many ways, for all people. If we live in a warm, spacious home, in a land that is fertile – not a wasteland – and we have light, clean air and water, then we have the foundation for real riches. To have, instead, the latest sound system, computer or calculator, and yet to breathe polluted air, is to be poor, from a witch's point of view. To have many exotic holidays abroad, yet not to be able to sunbathe in your own back garden without a protective cream to stop you getting skin cancer, is to be poor. To have a full food cupboard, yet to know that many of the items within it are laced with pesticides or are genetically modified, is to be poor. A witch knows that wealth is unspoiled food, clean air, an undamaged atmosphere, clean lakes and rivers where you can swim. Imagine that! A land in which all rivers and seas are safe to swim in, without the lurking threats of industrial pollution, untreated sewage or radioactivity. A land beneath a sky that shields us from harmful solar rays, a land rich with trees and wildflowers. This is wealth (though to a Pagan it seems like a mere birthright), and with wise planning and the use of nonabusive technology, it is perfectly congruent with motor transport, computers and material comfort (the perceived choice between environmentalism and a high standard of living being a cruel illusion).

At the moment, however, many of us need more cash, as well as the genuine wealth of a healthy environment. Being able to buy things is essential. Our Celtic ancestors did have a trading economy. The role of the merchant was important to them, for they traded gold and silver from Ireland, and tin

from Wales, the Mendips and Cornwall (among other things), to gain wine, pottery and coins from France. In many other parts of the world, beads or shells were used to represent money, to overcome the limitations of barter.

There has never been anything wrong with buying and selling done from need, not greed – not when the methods and merchandise harm none. Back then, as nowadays, people found that having wealth of some kind increased their possibilities of living adventurously. It could pay for a horse to take you on a long journey! It could purchase materials with which to make inspired artwork. If you had not enough mead to throw a party, you could buy some. Then, as now, money could purchase freedom from a constricting routine, as well as from anxiety.

When based in the Green economies that must become the entire Earth's future, we can have all the wealth that a wild rose has – and then some – to play and enrich our lives with, and to save against hard times. All it takes is the will to live from need, not greed and the vision to see that new solutions already exist to all the old problems.

Need not greed. A witch knows we need more than survival rations. We need books and music and travel. We need to give friends a meal without wondering how to pay the water rates or find money for our child's next school trip. We need to celebrate someone's birthday without experiencing a financial crisis! And we need all this in reward for work that can enhance life, causing no harm to nature. We need work that serves a real need in society, not a spurious one. And we all need to play roles, in our working lives, that are nonabusive. We need to do our unwaged work – as parents, caregivers, mystics, charity workers or whatever – in freedom from money worries. (Some of us are even still wondering why such work should be unwaged, but perhaps that is a disingenuous question in today's world.) We need to know that such wealth is available for the people in every land.

Wealth is a very physical issue, concerned with material justice. As such, it is a middle Earth matter. So the first prayers we say for wealth might be like this.

Prayer for Wealth for Everybody

Great Mother Earth and Green God of forests and all living beings, I invoke you. May your abundance and natural justice prevail for all of us. Help us to know how we may live in harmony with all the creatures and with one another, in wealth. Grant us all true riches – good food, a beautiful country that is healed of damage, and freedom from scarcity. May all the nature spirits have these riches. May all the animals, birds, fishes, insects and reptiles have these riches. May all the plants of each land have these riches. And may all we who need enough wealth for adventure and creativity have all these riches, as it harms none. So may all thrive and celebrate life! So may it be.

Such a prayer could be said in spring, around seed-planting time or on a waxing Moon, for maximum effect. However, if any prayer were being chosen to be said every day, all year round, or at any festival at all, then I would pick something like this, as it certainly deals with the most everyday concerns for us all. A ritual to follow this prayer could be a simple tending of a houseplant, or of plants in the garden, without any use of toxic materials. That is, you could repot something in organic compost or water it with spring water, saying, *Mother Earth and Green God, to you I now make this offering of care for plants. I give this plant what it needs. And may all receive abundance.*

The above is a statement of willingness to live by the principles we have invoked and not, as may at first appear, a demonstration to the deities of how we would like them to behave. It is, after all, we and not they who need to change our ways. But any small act of kindness, performed ritually, is an offering of ourselves as seed for the process of change.

At this point, many of us may be feeling that these rites for abundance and justice for all are a good idea and should certainly be done, but that meanwhile, we, ourselves, are flat broke and desperate! When that is the case, then serious rites for money must be done for the individual. Clearly, there are moral considerations. You want enough but you don't want your magic to rob someone else of what they may need, nor to cause harm of any kind. If such thoughts are not uppermost, then your magic could become another abusive 'technology' in a most greedy world. A wildwood mystic would be very aware of this, yet the financial worries may be severe. In such a case you need a rite which has genuine justice built into its structure. A prayer to the underworld deities and invocation of faerie assistance is one correct answer.

Faeries are not nature spirits, they are not flower devas, and they are not tiny. Many are about the same size as humans, according to the mystics, worldwide, who have seen them. But there are exceptions to this as the faerie realm contains all kinds of beings. They live in a different dimension from our own, one known as the other or underworld. Their business, partly, is to weave fate. They are also said to concern themselves with mortal affairs, through love, for purposes of guidance and initiation. Their world interpenetrates with ours, though to a lesser extent than in ancient times, so what affects us affects them and vice versa. The Dark Goddess and God – that is, they who rule over the subtle and hidden and unrevealed things – are the deities of the faerie realm (for a modern, in-depth examination of this subject, I recommend any of the books by R.J. Stewart on the faerie tradition). Faeries can nowadays mostly be met through psychic experiences and seen in visions. It is rare to see any signs of faerie existence with our physical eyes, though it can happen on rare occasions. I, myself, have been thus privileged.

Anyway, the main point about faeries, for the purposes of prosperity, is that they interest themselves in justice. If you pray to the Dark Goddess and God for faerie help, you can expect to get what is your right financially, but also to give what you owe. They are notorious, when invoked, for making sure that a person who has tried to wriggle out of her or his debts, will lose that money somehow. If you need money partly in order to settle debts, then you should tell them that you intend to pay up fairly. And if you have a genuine need for a lump sum or improved wages, and your cause is just, tradition says they will help you out. Natural justice is their concern, not human rules.

Prayer to Faerie Deities for Money

Deities of Faerie Realms, Goddess and God of Enchantment and Fate, I invoke you. As you watch over the balance between give and take, between want and necessity, be with me. Lady and Lord of the realm where there is song and poetry, wild lands and mystery, and also natural justice, I ask your blessing. Hear me call, from this, the mortal world. I need enough riches to [here list all the things that you want to do, e.g. pay all my debts, settle my bills in the future, bring up my children and pursue my vocation]. Please bring the money from those who have more than they need to me, who have not enough. Please bring it as gifts or as winnings or grants or patronage or as the right work opportunities, as it harms nobody. And, as the scales shall be balanced up, my fate is determined.

Have a small pair of scales on your altar, of the old-fashioned kind that use weights. Before you recite the prayer, have one side weighted down heavily. That represents the world. The empty side is yours. After the prayer, balance the two sides equally. Keep the scales on your altar for three cycles of the Moon. You should begin when the Moon is new.

If you prefer, you may scoop earth, representing wealth, from one full bowl to an empty one, until each holds the same. Keep these upon your altar, instead of scales.

Do not try to guess where your good fortune will come from. Never focus upon one particular possibility. From our limited perspective, we cannot know what is natural justice and what is not, and may make mistakes. But the faeries do know. We may leave it to them.

You may want to say the prayer at a known faerie haunt, e.g. a stone circle or other sacred site. It is customary to give the faeries an offering. Do not leave crystals or fruit and flowers by standing stones for them, as this will make the site feel cluttered to other visitors. Instead, you could offer to plant a tree in your garden or to feed the wild birds all winter, or something similar. Faeries are not nature spirits but they do need wild places, wild creatures and greenery, if ours is to be a world in which they can once again feel at home. For it is believed by some that although they could once live on our Earth and intermarry with mortals, they cannot now do so, because of the industrial revolution with all its noise and dirt. So, anything that heals the Earth or protects wild places is pleasing to them.

This also helps today's descendants of those half-human and half-faerie unions of the past. Many people are said to exist today who are of faerie stock and therefore cannot live healthily in a polluted world, or not so easily as people can who are of entirely human descent. This is not to say that all cases of 'decline' are due to the inheritance of faerie DNA, but some of them are. Nor does it mean that no one of such inheritance can survive urban stress, but it does mean that they will find it more difficult.

Faerie lore has been explored the most in the Celtic lands – Ireland, Scotland, the Isle of Man, Wales, Cornwall and Brittany. But other countries, from Egypt to Australia, from Italy to North America, have faerie teachings or traditions of faerie presences, in some form or another. In fact, they appear to be known about in every continent.

You may now be wondering why there are not lots of obviously wealthy witches around, if we only have to ask the faeries for assistance in order to get money. Well, part of the answer is that the above spells will not necessarily make you very rich. They should simply mean that you have enough, which most of us do, somehow or other. When our money problems become severe, it is because we have forgotten to ask, being too 'away with the faeries' to have thought about it.

Wild places far from the towns, deserted beaches, hilltops or woodlands are the best places for visions of faerie folk. However, if you are stuck inside a city, you can still say the prayer for wealth, anyway. Prayers and spells cross time and space easily.

When the money arrives, say thank you. But please note, this spell will only work if your cause is just, as the faeries do not help us otherwise.

Grace for Prosperity

I give thanks to the Goddess and God of the Faerie Realms for money. I give thanks for [here name your good fortune]. May I be guided by faerie familiars to use such wealth as I have wisely and generously, that my gold shall not turn into lumps of coal because of bad dealings. Nor my money become as dry leaves.

The upperworld may not seem to have much to do with money. Yet sun deities have always been invoked in rites of wealth, and traditionally, people turn over the coins in their pockets on seeing the new moon, as this is said to bring increase. The following prayer is an example of one to the sun deities, but you can say it to the Sun Goddess or God alone, if you prefer to.

Prayer to the Sun Goddess and God for Wealth

Great Lady and Lord of the Golden Realms of warmth and light, I invoke your assistance. You ripen corn and bring good things to flourish. Yours is the light of our summer ease and joyfulness, when we enjoy good times. Grant to me a time of prosperity, a time that's 'in the Sun'. Banish from my life the shadows of poverty. As it harms none, let me come into a golden time, when I have all I really need. As I share with others, without greed, let wealth come to me.

This rite is a good one to do at the midsummer solstice. Place something gold on your altar: a piece of jewelry, a golden charm from a bracelet or – if all else fails – a golden foil chocolate wrapper.

Now make a vow to take on some task that means giving to somebody else a more golden time. This may mean sponsoring a child's education in a third-world country, through a charity like 'Save the Children'; adopting a homeless cat; working in a charity shop for a few mornings per week, or something of the sort. As with the offering to earth deities, this is not meant to show the Goddess or God what to do for us, but to align ourselves with the energy of giving – and receiving. As witches say, what you give out, you receive, three times increased. As a motivation for helping others, this may seem a little cheap, but to be pragmatic about it, everyone benefits. Having said that, the spell still works best if you give what comes naturally. In other words, it is better to adopt a cat, or sponsor a dolphin, if that appeals to you, than to volunteer to work for a charity, if that does not.

All this is a far cry from the public's idea of black magic rites for money, involving orgies and cruelty to goats (I'm afraid the above rites may seem rather dull in comparison!).

10 Prayers and Spells for Good Fortune

In the Scandinavian tradition, the Goddess of Fate – or luck – is a Triple Goddess, called the Norns, who presides over a sacred well, beneath the world tree. As such, she is an underworld Goddess. In the Celtic tradition, also, the Fate Goddess is connected with water. Magical lands beneath the waves, or islands across water, were said to be the home of the fate-weaving faeries. This may be because in her upperworld aspect, the Fate Goddess is linked with the Moon, and Moon and water are always seen as being connected, especially Moon and ocean. For the Moon's magnetic power creates the tides of the earthly seas and also rules over the tides of fortune. The Moon, wishing wells, the tides that ebb and flow and the spinning, weaving or cutting of something are all linked with 'Lady Luck', in European belief. As Morgan Le Fey (or La Fate), what she and her assistant faeries weave is the soul of life, which can be seen, psychically, as a dream picture, as though reflected in water. And, as explained before, the faeries weave partly with what we give them. They weave in our feelings and attitudes, high ideals or unresolved conflicts. They weave in our links with one another and the lessons we choose to learn. This, in turn, creates our future. If our aspirations are noble, it helps. They can work with bright threads then, to make a much better picture.

When looking at issues of feeling and meaning, this is what we see – the dream picture that is made in the underworld. On the other hand, when looking at the tapestry of fate from the point of view of middle Earth matters, many psychics see a vast web of light, a three-dimensional and cosmic web. We are all placed on this, somewhere, and through it we are linked to all living beings, and also to the Moon and stars and Sun; in fact, to all of creation. This middle Earth vision shows clearly how we are all part of one huge organism (the Universe), and that we are each affected by, and affecting, all else that lives.

In the upperworld reaches, where the Moon holds sway, and where we can 'read our fate in the stars' as astrologers, the issue is how we respond to concepts like 'eternity', and what we make of the great and eternal themes, like love and parent–child relationships and the search for meaningful work. Ideally, how do we think these things should be? How should life be lived, collectively, for peace and justice? And how well will we stand by our ideals? Will we be prepared to adapt them, if they prove false or wrong? Upperworld aspirations are reflected in the soul weaving done by the faeries, just as the Moon or stars may be seen reflected in a lake or shining on the sea, but they are lived out in middle Earth.

The Witch Goddess of Fate, however we name her, is she of Moon and stars and Earth and water, the upperworld, middle Earth and underworld. By her, we can attempt to heal our fortune, when we have gone astray from the best destiny that is possible. It is by her, also, and by the God, that we can read fate and try to understand destiny, through divination.

There is no 'Lord Luck' that I know of. The deity of fate has always, traditionally, been a Goddess. However, the God can reveal destiny, and also change it – and he can bestow blessings and avert evil. I do not know why luck is female. Cynics might say it is because men have perceived women as fickle, just like fate appears to be. More profoundly, it may be because women weave the genetic material, that shapes our destiny in a very basic way, inside our bodies, during pregnancy. So we might well say that the feminine force, the Goddess, is the prime fate weaver. But the God, the great cosmic magician, also has work to do. In nature, he brings genetic diversity, and in life, generally, he challenges us to experiment and to increase creativity.

In fact, the Goddess and God are one, being simply the polar opposites on a continuum of divinity. So 'Lord Luck'

does exist, in fact? Perhaps more as a 'bolt from the blue' than as the settled outcome of obvious causes. As a woman, I feel comfortable praying to the Goddess for clairvoyant and fate-weaving power, and to the God for the power to realize my best destiny. A man might prefer a different approach, but these are individual matters.

The main thing to understand is that the faerie realm, the underworld, is where the business of fate gets most attention. It is here that Moon and stars (or ideals) are reflected, and here that causes are woven into our soul picture that make our life on Earth. The Goddess is queen of all fate in this realm, and the God is a prophet, like the Celtic Bran, or like Merlin or Odin, and a healer of destiny. They will both help us, if we ask them. We can say prayers like these – first, to the Goddess.

Prayer to the Faerie Queen Goddess for Good Fortune

Goddess of Fate, Faerie Queen Goddess, I now invoke you. Lady who ordains the ebb and flow of every tide and the wine in the cup of life, and the work of faerie fate weavers, I call upon you. Help me to sense my own fate clearly, to understand the signs, to divine meaning. May faerie helpers, in your name, bring good opportunities. So may my luck increase, that my life may serve life, my happiness and good fortune to be shared with many.

Wear something green, the faeries' color, when you say this prayer. Next, write the faeries a letter. Tell them that you need a change of luck, so that you may be well placed enough to be creative. If you feel you have had bad luck in love or about money or any matter, then mention that especially, asking for a change to good fortune. It is always best to write to them about just one subject at a time.

Now describe in detail the life that you want to live, the life-serving things that you plan to do, when you have better luck. With whom would you share your good fortune? Tell the faeries about them, too. What plans do you have for creative projects? How could you help people around you, or the land or the creatures, if you had better luck? What are the exciting and life-enhancing things you would do?

Do not be too specific about the form your improved luck should take. Do not tell the faeries, for instance, where your home should be, or who could be your new lover or how you should make more money. They know far better than we, how things can work out for the best. Just tell them what you need, and leave them room for maneuver.

Finally, make them a promise: 'If this comes to be, I will . . .' (for example, if asking for better luck about housing) 'always be hospitable/give a home to a stray animal/make of my home a temple' or whatever is appropriate for you. This is not a bribe for the faeries, but a way of pledging to share what comes to you. It is the 'sacrifice', the offering, that is part of a traditional spellcasting. Besides, the faeries give out luck to those who will pass it on – they really, really do not like hoarders. Remember, however, you must keep your promise, if the luck is not to run out.

Spells like the above have a childlike quality, rather like writing to Father Christmas, but it is the innocence and the simplicity of them which brings the power. In this instance, leave the letter in your garden overnight, at full moon (or on a balcony or windowsill, if you feel that would seem more private – or if you don't have a garden). In the morning, retrieve it, so that its contents remain secret, known only to you and the faeries. Do not show it to anyone.

If your household is large and busy, so that you cannot guarantee that your spell will remain unnoticed by others, then you can bury the letter, instead. This is like delivering it into the earth, so that the faeries who are underground, in hollow hills, will be able to find it. Try to use the most earth-friendly materials for a letter that you mean to bury – preferably unbleached recycled paper, and, if you can manage it, biodegradable ink made with blackcurrant juice or red wine, perhaps thickened with a little cornstarch or cocoa, or something similar. You can then use a dip pen, as calligraphers do, to write the letter. Alternatively, you could use a pencil. All this extra care and attention is troublesome, but it does boost the magic.

This is a most beautiful spell to do if you are camping somewhere that is remote from all cities, some wild and green place, where faeries gather. To leave your letter outside in the full moonlight in such a place as that could be an experience to remember.

Can the faeries read? Yes, because to them, all language is magical. All early writing systems were developed for magic and ritual purposes. They know that to write is a sacred act. They do not like some of the uses to which letters have been put in the present-day human world – as currency for mind manipulation and all manner of other desecrations, which have debased words altogether. But they know and understand writing. In any case, the letter's contents will be made known to them, telepathically, as you are writing it. The real point of the writing and the leaving of the letter in the moonlight or underground, is that it makes it a ritual act, one that makes such contact possible on psychic levels.

What is luck? Many say it is the art of being in the right place at the right time, or the knack of making the most of our opportunities. This is largely true, though not, of course, the entire story. Another popular piece of folk wisdom is that 'we make our own luck'. This is a vital piece of information, for it tells us that our own positive attitudes, a psychological readiness to be fortunate, as well as an instinctive sensing of which are the good opportunities, make all the difference.

Many of us feel we don't deserve good luck. Conscious or unconscious guilt about past wrongdoing (whether real or imagined) keeps many of us believing we deserve a hard time. Then there is the issue of what really is lucky, in the long run. To take an obvious example, a job loss can appear a real piece of ill fortune, at first. But, if it leads to a new and happier life, it is actually lucky. It may force a career change that leads to a more fulfilled existence. Some things are blessings in disguise. More subtly, even genuinely bad experiences can lead us to wisdom or increased compassion for others, through understanding suffering. There may be lessons more valuable than gold, in many difficult experiences, though we may not see it at the time. However, some suffering is pointless. The faerie fate weavers do not want us to have lives of dreary, sad deprivation. They want us to learn and grow, yes, but they want us to flourish.

How do we tell which life events are gifts, or even just plain unavoidable, and which are instances of settling for less than we need? Sometimes, if we're spoilt, we may complain a lot, even when given a lucky break others would love to have (the 'it's not quite good enough' syndrome). At other times, we may not have realized that our 'good luck' is only the icing on a stale and disgusting cake.

All this can be really confusing, but we can pray for guidance, by saying something like this.

Prayer to the Faerie God for Understanding of Fortune

Wise Lord who helps us to steer our lives by the stars, God of the Crystal Boat and Crystal Tower, I call to you. Guide all upon the Earth to a good destiny of increased wisdom and fulfilled love. Grant to me to understand my own fate, and to know what is right and good in my life, and what is not. To know what I need and what I should accept with gratitude – and what to avoid. Enhance in me the understanding of what my good fortune is, and how to use it. May I be in harmony with the true needs of all, and so fulfill my best destiny.

When the above prayer is answered, through a dream or a psychic reading, or just as a sudden realization, a new light is shed upon old problems. Sit or lie quietly after saying it, and see if you can feel the answers. But do not worry if you cannot. It is very usual for the guidance to come unexpectedly.

To return to the subject of fate itself, as woven, we can gain a good understanding by relating it to the real structure of a cloth or tapestry. There are two kinds of thread in material and also in our lives – the warp and the weft. The ones that go across the loom to make the picture are called the weft. These may be changed often, bringing in new colors, making a (hopefully) good design. They are what we are handed as we go along through life, opportunities of many kinds – relationships, education, work possibilities, gifts, travel options and so on. Some may be far better than they, at first, seem. Yet others are mistakes in fancy packaging. We can choose some and discard others. We are not all handed a good thick bundle of these, and we are not all handed threads of the same quality. The fact remains, some folks get given many fabulous threads, gold and silver, and still make a terrible mess of their life picture. Others are given quite a limited range of what seem to be dull colors, yet still make a picture that is beautiful and speaks to all of us. This is the extent to which we 'make our own luck' – by using what life hands us, wisely or adventurously, and with imagination.

Then there are the other threads, the warp ones. These go along the loom, as the foundation of any design. They are what can't be changed, the things we don't choose but must work with or around, like it or not: for example, the socio-economic conditions of the country where we live, or the attitudes and characters of our parents. Arguably, we may have chosen these before being born, for the sake of life lessons or of what we wanted to achieve, but not a lot can be done about them once we are born. Many things come into this category. The country where we live may be at war or peace, in a state of famine, or of increase. There may be an especially cold winter, or long-term climate changes may be going to occur. Laws may be passed which cause stress or unhappiness throughout most of the nation, or there may be a time of liberality. Our parents, or somebody else close to us, may suddenly die, or they may live long or become rich and famous. All these things are outside our own control. They are the given things. We cannot choose whether to experience them or not. We can, however, choose what we will make of them, how we will react, and so on.

These longwise warp threads quite clearly demonstrate that the picture of our own life is actually a detail within the big tapestry that is all life. They show us more clearly than the weft threads may do that we are all connected with one another, and with the fate of Earth herself. For example, if the South American economies continue to do badly, it is more likely that what remains of the rainforests will be chopped down. This will affect Earth's atmosphere for us all. Closer to home, you may have a neighbor who likes to play loud music late at night, and is deaf to 'please turn it down'. This means that your family may suffer from increased stress and poor sleep, with repercussions the next day. Events ripple out. The luck of one person, or country, is ours as well, for good or ill. What affects one, affects us all. The best thing that we can do about this is to pray for good fortune, an increase in blessings, for all beings. All blessings and well-wishings improve the luck of others, or of the land (according to what we bless) and, from the point of view of a wildwood mystic, these may be some of the best prayers that we can say. As the general level of well-being increases, so do each of us live in a more relaxed, generous world – and this is undoubtedly good fortune. Such prayers may be requests to the deities to grant good luck. Or, as in the following example, we may ourselves give the blessing, in their names.

Prayer to the Deities of Middle Earth for Good Fortune/World Blessing

Great Lady and Lord of the Web of Light that links us all, we are your creation. In your names, I bless us all, I bless all creation. Especially, today, I bless ____ [here name your family, friends or any person/creature/place in need of a blessing]. May all good fortune be theirs. May their happiness increase.

Such blessings are a very important part of a witch's work. They are good to say on a hilltop, on a bright sunny day, or at any peak time when you are feeling good. The summer solstice is an ideal time for them, but anywhere, anytime, will do. Touch the ground when you have said any general blessing – place one hand, palm down, upon the earth.

Of course, you can say a specific blessing for just one place, person or being of any kind, rather than a world blessing that includes the specific. In that instance, you might (if possible) place your hand lightly upon the person or place or creature or object. But if blessing someone from a distance, you may just project your thought toward them, as though touching them in spirit.

Finally, upon the subject of fate, we have to remember that

it is our ideals (or lack of them) which shape our lives, perhaps most of all. In illustration of this, if the highest ideal that we have is to live in the most luxury we can acquire, then we may have a very comfortable life, but our life tapestry won't be very inspiring! And obviously, we, ourselves, may end up feeling unfulfilled, empty and frightened inside, as though it were all meaningless. Ideals are connected with upperworld matters. This is the realm of the high elves (the Shining Ones, long known to Celtic ancestors and others worldwide), whom the Church refer to as angels. These beings guide us in respect of the larger view of life, rather than just comfort and ease. They inspire us to take risks, to serve a creative vision, to find answers to the world's problems – or, at least, to try. How we respond to them is always reflected in the soul weaving or life picture, created by the underworld faeries.

Prayer to the Upperworld Deities of Higher Purposes

Great Lady and Lord of the Upperworld, the starry heavens, I call upon you. From olden times you have shown us a sense of the sacred and lifted our minds above the mundane – away from our own troubles. Bless us all with an increased understanding of more than just our own lives. For myself, I ask to see clearly how I may aspire to serve an ideal. Let the winged beings, the shining ones, who are your messengers, now visit me in sleep and give me knowledge of what I may live for. And how to let my fate serve higher purposes.

This prayer may be said last thing at night, before you go to sleep. It is even better if you can be outside, gazing up at the stars, in some quiet country place, and then say it.

You can, of course, pray to the Goddess or God, as guide to destiny, in every aspect of the entire world tree, on every level. You can say something like this.

Prayer to the Fate Goddess of Upperworld, Middle Earth and the Underworld

> *Great Goddess of Fate, Lady of Moon and stars and the web of light in the Earth and woven waters, I call upon you to guide us all. Help us return into harmony with nature's tides, which reveal the tides of fate. Help us fulfill our best destiny. Show us, by your messengers, the nature spirits and faeries who come in guiding dreams, or walk with us on the lonely road, what our best fate might be. Guide each of us to walk our path in wisdom. I ask you especially to show me/my friend ____ [name them] the truth of ____ [state the question]. Let me/her/him decide in truth and beauty.*

This kind of prayer can be said before giving a psychic reading to anyone, perhaps using the tarot cards or runes or dreamstones, or any other system of divination. It can also be said before going to sleep, in request for a guiding dream.

Tradition tells us that what may be used to read fate (the runes, Celtic tree cards etc.), may also be used to heal or reweave it. For example, in a reading showing a forthcoming illness, other cards/stones etc. may be added to the spread, bringing a protective and healing influence. Or, the symbols for illness may be removed altogether, and replaced with others showing creative life changes. If this is done with a prayer to the Lady and Lord of Good Fortune, to let this fate be changed for the better, according to your spell, then bad events may be averted (that is, unless they are what must come to be, for what the peoples of the East call 'karmic' reasons. Even then, your spell may soften the blow).

11 How to Create Magical Prayers

If you are a born wildwood mystic, a person with the spirit of enchantment strong in you, then you will want to create your own prayers – to the Earth, Moon, Sun, Star or Underworld Goddesses or Gods, or to the Great Goddess or Great God, meaning the universal, divine powers around the whole world tree. You may already have been saying things like, *Please guide me, Moon Goddess*, or *Please bless* ____ [a friend] or *Thank you for my freedom, Horned God.* If you are new to all this, then you may want to begin in just such a way – saying prayers which are that simple. In any case, however experienced, we all resort to one-line spontaneous prayers, from time to time. They are heartfelt and natural.

In moving to what is more complex, you could find it useful to adapt prayers from this book, or to say them just as they are. Sooner or later, however, you will want to create your own fresh ones, formal and structured for magical potency. So how is it done?

The most important thing to remember is always to start any prayer with an invocation. This means a summoning up, within yourself, by using a 'word picture' of an image of the deity. Your image may include symbols – like a crescent Moon, or wild deer, or a forest or ocean – as well as qualities. You may have a series of places, animals, plants or abstract ideas. The important thing is that these represent to you the nature of the Goddess or God to whom you are praying. This is much less difficult than it sounds. You may, for example, wish to pray to a Goddess of Love, but not know her traditional names or associations (though she has many – among other names, to the Celts she is Rhiannon, to the Nordic peoples, the Goddess Freya, to the witches of the Middle Ages, Marian). Without any knowledge, you can still invoke her easily. Begin by saying *Great Goddess of Love, Lady of . . .* and then add all the things that mean love to you: *Lady of hearts, flowers and deep embraces, Lady of the heart's fulfillment, Great Lady of happiness. . . .*

If you want to pray to the God of Nature about an environmental matter, you do not have to know that, to our ancestors, he was called Cernnunos or Herne. You can just say, *God of wild animals and all wild places, please hear me. I call to you as the guardian of all that's living and of nature's balance.*

This easily you can invoke a Goddess or God. You can build up an image and a feeling for them, inside you, by just describing them and their domain (their sphere of activity). The more descriptive words and phrases you add to your invocation, the stronger it becomes. But it is better to choose a few symbols you are sure of, and repeat them more than once, chanting them, than to confuse yourself looking for new ideas, if they don't come easily.

In the above example, the key words are 'guardian', 'wild animals and wild places' and 'nature's balance'. By simply repeating a sentence containing these, you can begin to conjure up a feeling for what such a guardian is actually like. In other words, you will invoke the God within you. The purpose of such invocations is that they provide a link between ourselves and the divine powers, who are far greater than we are. By invoking the God or Goddess within, we can awaken our own connection with the deities – although they transcend our own existence. This is not because they are archetypal aspects of our own psychology – they are far, far more than that, being creatrix and co-creator of all that is. Describing them turns the attention of our spirits toward them, as well as awakening the numinousness within ourselves. There is then immediate contact. It is hard to put this into words. Being mystery, it must be experienced to be understood.

Anyway – rule number one about magical prayer – begin with an invocation, a description of the Goddess or God and of their powers. Do not try to make it poetic. Just use words or phrases that seem accurate, and any images from nature that easily connect with your theme. The deity that you describe is what you will contact, however you name them.

Many Christians have invoked a fierce, intolerant and jealous God, one in whose name they have burned witches, denied women's sexuality and massacred tribespeople to destroy indigenous religions. They did all this in the name of Jesus. Since it is impossible to imagine the benign healer of the New Testament would ever approve such behavior, we can only conclude that they had not invoked Jesus, but an evil counterfeit instead. The lesson is clear to us all, whatever our faith: deity names do not matter, however holy they appear to be, in comparison to the attributes we decide to pin on to that name.

Having described any deity's goodness in (as befits a witch or Pagan mystic) entirely wild, primal terms, you will have made the right start to any prayer. After that, it's hard to go wrong. But what are the next stages? Sometimes you don't need to worry about them. Some very magical and potent prayers are said spontaneously, without structure. A formal prayer will be constructed in steps or stages – three of them – but a prayer that is sudden and heartfelt may only ramble but still be effective. This is because it makes up in raw sincerity what it lacks in finesse. It is still vital to begin with a clear invocation, however brief, for this is what makes it more than a desperate inner monologue. The turning of the witch's attention toward the Goddess or God is what brings an alteration in consciousness, making it possible for us really to communicate with realms of spirit. This attunes us to eternal realities which transcend our fears and all the little ways that we limit magic.

The next stage after the invocation is simply to state a request (or to make a thanksgiving – but unless the prayer is a grace, it is usually a case of asking for something). If the prayer is a formal one, written out to be learned by heart and spoken many times, then we have a chance to think carefully about what we're asking for. This may be inner guidance, a healing, a blessing for the land, a good love relationship, or a banishing of depression, or anything else that is constructive. Fairly obviously, it is better if the subject is within the deity's especial province. This does not matter if you are addressing the Great Goddess, Mother of All Living, she who includes all Goddesses within her infinite being – or the Great God. Since these are the universal divine powers, you can pray to them about anything. However, people can find that praying to a specific deity feels less abstract and impersonal.

It helps to address the appropriate Goddess or God for your particular concerns. Most formal magical rites rest upon this premise. It may seem too obvious to mention, but you would not normally ask Aphrodite, Goddess of Love, for money. Nor Persephone, Queen of the Dead, for love. Nor Manannan, God of Deep Truth and Transformation, for a new home. However, people do forget this.

As a matter of fact, the rule is not inflexible. Pagan deities are not exactly like Christian patron saints, assigned to particular realms of concern. They are mystery and full of paradox; they are inclusive, vital. So a request for prosperity to Cernunnos, Guardian of Nature, is not quite like asking St. Francis for a fat bank account! Our Goddesses and Gods cannot ever be fitted into psychic pigeonholes. Therefore, seasoned witches and mystics may well decide to address their prayers to a deity not usually approached for such a

matter – and do it successfully. If they have made a lifelong devotion to one deity in particular, a self-dedication, then they may pray about almost everything to that one Goddess or God, aware that the prayers will be answered in terms of that deity's resonance. However, these are matters for the experienced. If you are just beginning as a wildwood mystic, it is best to address your prayers for love to the Love Goddess or God, those for prosperity to the Goddess and God of Abundance and so on (on all three levels of the world tree).

Stage three of creating a prayer is normally a consecration of the matter. It is what might be called the offering or 'sacrifice'. This makes the issue a sacred one. By dedicating it to divine purposes in some way, it is set apart from everyday power games or human foolishness or desecration – and linked with the common good. It is lifted beyond the normal push and shove of human striving, and also it is bound only to work out if it serves the good purpose to which it has been connected. Thus, a witch's prayers have a built-in safety mechanism, ensuring that the magic which follows (if magic is to be done) can only be successful if it harms no one and, in fact, enhances life. This is most easily explained by an example.

Stage One – Invocation

I call upon the Lady of Love, Lady of Romance and deep fulfillment, you who bless all true lovers with happiness.

Stage Two – Statement (of request)

Please bless my friend _____ [name them] with the right love relationship.

Stage Three – Consecration (the offering)

Let that love serve her/his best interests and those of her/his future partner, and may it be a source of harmony. May it serve life by creating an atmosphere of joy that lifts people's spirits.

The love that has been prayed for has thus been consecrated to divine purposes.

Most of the prayers in this book are complex or expanded versions of the above formula. This is based in traditional spellcraft and ritual practices, in which there is normally an invocation of the Goddess or God (or both), a statement of intention or of the purpose of the ritual, and a consecration or offering of the materials used in the magic, and of the successful outcome of the enchantment – or of something arising from it. Another example could be this one.

Stage One – Invocation

Mother Earth, Lady of Abundance, you who provide for all creatures, I call upon you.

Stage Two – Statement (of request)

I ask you to give me prosperity. May all my needs be met for goods and money. Without greed, I ask to have enough and to have security.

Stage Three – Consecration

And may my future prosperity and well-being serve the environment, in balance, in deep ecology.

This prayer would need to be preceded by careful thought. How would such an offering be carried out in practice? All your environmentally-caring deeds and purchases would be ways of honoring it. But also, your life could change unexpectedly, so that you became, for example, an ecowarrior of some kind or a person who created a wildlife sanctuary. The point about magic is that it is mystery – not like a business transaction but like love.

Another example would be this one:

Stage One – Invocation

Great God of Doorways and Thresholds, Oak God, I call upon you as God of the Forest Pathways and of Herbal Wisdom.

Stage Two – Statement (request and thanksgiving)

I ask you to grant me knowledge of herbal magic. Teach me to safely work with plants for magical purposes. Let me know how to speak with all plant spirits, and how to read the future, by herbal auguries. And what plants to bring to the altar to make my spells strong. I thank you for the knowledge I already have. I thank you for all wild woods.

Stage Three – Consecration

Let all my old and new knowledge bring guidance and increased well-being for many. Let it make me a more effective wisewoman/wiseman. Let it do no harm to any wild place nor to any person but let it serve life.

It is easy to see how a planned prayer makes an ideal start and focus for any spellcraft. In the above, for instance, the invocation suggests where to do the work (why not go out and find a woodland and pray beneath an actual oak tree?), and then the medium for the spell (how about consecrating an oak twig or acorn, as a link with the Oak God, and carrying it everywhere you go?).

In the first example, the prayer for love, ideas that spring to mind include filling a chalice with wine (because of the word 'fulfillment' and because of the traditional association of cups and happiness), and blessing it with the words, 'May she/he who drinks this, drink also of the wine of fulfillment in love.' Then, offer it to your friend if she/he is willing.

If you bear in mind the three stages of magical prayer – the invocation, the statement, the consecration – then it is easy to construct a prayer about any matter. When you take advice from a familiar spirit about the prayer and resulting spellcraft, it is even easier (but more about that in the next chapter).

You may be wondering how your invocations can be made to relate to the three levels of the world tree. That is quite straightforward, too.

It is clear that all deities have an upperworld, middle Earth and underworld aspect. Take the Love Goddess, known to the Greeks as Aphrodite. She is associated with the planet Venus, romance, erotic fulfillment on a sensual level, and with the seas, or tides of fate, that bring people together. (Love can, of course, create or seal our fate.) Therefore, we can pray to her as 'Great Goddess of Love . . .' including her aspects in each of the three realms. Or we can say 'Great Goddess of Love, I call to you as' (for example) 'Lady of middle Earth.' This is if we want to pray to her about a physical matter, to do with sexual love or fertility.

Similarly, with each Goddess or God, we can include in

our prayer the words 'Lady/Lord of the upperworld/middle Earth/underworld', if it is appropriate to be specific. Or simply pray to 'Great Goddess/God of . . .' if it is not.

This may seem impossible if the deity is especially linked with one realm, as in the case of the British Sun Goddess, Sulis, who seems, on the face of it, to be entirely of the upperworld. But Sulis is also the Sun at midnight – that is, the Sun in the underworld. To underline her underworld aspect, she is Goddess of the hot mineral waters that rise in Bath as a sacred spring. This makes her a goddess of prophecy and healing. In addition, she is Harvest Mother, as her named sanctuary Silbury Hill indicates, rising, as it does, from a fertile landscape and being a traditional place to celebrate the ripening of the crops.

The Celtic God Manannan is primarily a God of the sea, and linked with faerie realms. However, he is said to have a three-spoked wheel on which he travels through the sky. He is also active upon the land, transforming people's lives.

The Horned God Cernunnos/Herne leads the wild hunt through the night sky (or upperworld) as he collects the spirits of the newly dead, to take them to the summerlands. Yet he is known as protector of the wild places of middle Earth. He resides in the faerie realm, the underworld. His Welsh counterpart, Gwyn ap Nudd, is the same.

Any Goddess or God is, essentially, mystery, and active anywhere, everywhere, thus containing aspects in each of the three realms (in the case of Moon Goddesses like Morgan Le Fey, three aspects in each of the three realms). But you do not have to know traditional Goddess or God names to be a wildwood mystic. If you are in the west of England, Wales or Brittany (or many other places as well), and you pray to the Goddess of Fate, then clearly the Faerie Goddess, Morgan, will know who you mean. And you can call to her as Moon Goddess in the upperworld, or as the inner spirit of the land, with its healing springs and wells in middle Earth, or as the Sea Goddess and Faerie Queen, whose realm is below land level. In fact, if you are in another continent, you can still pray to the Fate Goddess and be heard by Morgan – for you may have ancestral links with one of her sacred places, or have spent former lives in her service. The same is true of all other Goddesses and Gods. And you do not need to use names if you do not want to. If you are a beginner, you can say things like, 'I call upon the God of Wisdom in the underworld', and leave it that simple.

Underworld matters are things like psychology, emotions, inner meanings, past life or soul links, buried causes, the arts, a sense of the sacred, purification, deep, transformational healing, fate, prophecy, death, rebirth, regeneration, all psychic senses, the past, ancestral memories and teachings, the faeries, and the deep or profound self.

Middle Earth matters are about our relationship with the land, and with all creatures, physically as well as spiritually, about nature, animals, physical harmony and justice, nature spirits, manifestation of our ideas and plans, practicality, sensuality, the body, trees, flowers and all herbs, minerals, gardening, farming, homemaking, crafts, beauty, abundance, well-being, the countryside, the continuum of all life, environmentalism, the natural or instinctual self and the conscious mind.

Upperworld matters are about the overview, long-term repercussions, events that affect whole sections of the community or all of us, the Universe, cosmic tides, ideals, compassion, aspirations, expanded consciousness, exaltation, divine messages, the big picture (including other galaxies), transcendence, the transpersonal, metaphysics, and the higher self.

These are the working rules. However, it is often helpful, when dealing with a matter that seems stuck, or unresolvable, to direct your prayers to another realm than the obvious choice, or to each in turn, as in the previous chapters on health, wealth and good fortune.

12 Help from a Familiar Spirit

In this chapter, we shall look at the practice of gaining help in the construction of prayers and spells from familiar spirits. For these give inspiration and ideas, rather than just the technical aspect.

A natural witch, a hedge witch, sooner or later meets with guides or helpers, who are from Pagan spirit realms. These are our familiar spirits. Stereotypically, they have been depicted as almost always cats or toads, who live with the witch and assist her or him psychically.

Of course, many witches have always had pets who help them in spirit realms. We still do. Sometimes, this has a practical aspect. Toads, for example, are the gardener's friend, eating up ants and other pests that might have damaged the plants. The village wisewoman or wiseman of the past, or today's herbalist, with a garden full of healing herbs, could well find the toad to be a good helper. As for cats, many people have kept them, and still do, to rid their homes of mice. Country living, and dilapidated country dwellings, could mean mice were in and out of your kitchen regularly. The cat is good company, as well. Many people talk to their cats, regarding them as a close (perhaps the closest) friend. There is no reason why this companionship should not extend into psychic realms.

However, many witches work with nature spirits who do

not live with them (or at least not in a body) and who are not pets. Our familiars in middle Earth may be nature spirits of any kind: animal spirits from any species (birds, snakes, lizards etc.), tree spirits and even spirits of places.

Familiar spirits can also be underworld contacts, in which case they are of the faerie realm or are wise ancestors who want to guide us.

Needless to say, whether physically present or not, and of whatever type, we do not feed them on our own blood!

The practice of gaining these allies in the spirit realm goes back a long, long way. Shamanic healers – those palaeolithic and neolithic ancestors of today's witches, and of all magical practitioners – developed a strong relationship with spirit guides, through their sensitivity to nature, and in 'inner plane' journeyings. Cave paintings, old tales and present-day tribal teachings all show that the art of friendship with familiars was once taken for granted, as the essence of magical work. In Britain, the Celtic tribes had what, in deference to the Native American tradition, we now call 'totem animals', believed to give clan members assistance. European tradition also contains the mythology of being led or assisted in a quest by a particular animal. Some of these are faerie beings, like the white hart or white horse so often associated with the faerie queen. In fact, Celtic mythology contains many faerie beasts – faerie hounds (white with red ears), faerie pigs, faerie cattle etc., and, of course, references to the faeries themselves, as encountering, confronting, guiding or helping (or enticing away) the hero or heroine. Well-known faerie tales show the same kind of thing. Cinderella has a faerie Goddessmother, the elves help the shoemaker in the Brothers Grimm's fairytale. The faeries bless or curse (or amend the curse) in *Sleeping Beauty*.

Of course, many of the above examples are not familiar spirits, in the sense of personal spirit friends or guides or helpers, but they do show the ancestral importance of contact with Pagan spirits.

My own lifelong familiar spirit is a faerie woman. She is very beautiful, black-haired, almost as tall as I am and has webbed feet – a far cry from the dainty, little, gauzy flower faeries of Victorian literature (but the faerie realm contains all types). I have one other constant companion, a sea bird, who is a marvellous spirit healer and a skilled purifier, psychically speaking, of places – and of my own aura.

Of course, most of us witches owe a great deal to our familiars. As wildwood mystics, we become increasingly aware of the presence of spirits of all kinds. But as witches, we learn to work with them, utilizing the wildwood mystic's sensitivity, for healing or inspirational purposes. Through them, we may gain guidance on how to word our prayers or spells, and how to enact rites of all kinds. As for myself, I would hardly dream of doing any important piece of ritual magic without consulting my familiars first. The faerie woman has inspired most of my writing. As a team, we answer each other's need, for we would both like to see sound Pagan teachings becoming more widespread on Earth. I am her 'portal' out to the Earth level in this respect. In return, she assists me in what I want to do and to know, magically.

Familiars also give psychic protection, healing, and guidance on the future, if asked to. They will not, of course, live our lives for us, taking all challenges and risks away. The life of a witch is, after all, meant to be developmental. How could we gain psychic, psychological or spiritual strength if everything was done for us? However, a familiar is a true, magical friend and the greatest help.

Dictionary definitions of the word 'familiar' include, among other things, 'demon attending and obeying witch etc.'. I'm sure none of my spirit friends would appreciate being called 'demon' – how rude! But they do 'attend' witches. The word is also defined as 'intimate, in close friendship', and this is correct. The relationship is one of mutual respect and friendliness. We do not command our familiars, and they do not obey us (nor we them).

As for the story about feeding familiars upon blood, I think we may safely assume this was a Church-devised horror story, designed to put people off the Old Religion. What is true, however, is that there is an exchange of subtle and psychic energy between the witch and the familiar. The witch provides the kind of energy that borders between the psychic and the physical, and is called 'etheric' (there is masses of this

kind of energy available to us in wild places and by the sea, which is why many spirits prefer to meet us there). This enables some kind of manifestation to take place, such as your familiar being able to talk to you telepathically or even, on more rare occasions, appear before you, if only as a wavering shape. Sometimes, in my own experience, there can be lovely smells, like essential oils or fresh flowers, around the house for no physical reason. This can occur when a familiar wishes to signal encouragement, or to give healing to you or to someone else.

I have wondered what it is, specifically, that a witch's familiar gets out of the job, aside from being able to affect the manifest world. When I asked mine, she said, 'We get the same satisfaction that a human teacher, counselor or healer gets from their work. It is fulfilling. Also, we like receiving affection. It is that simple.'

'Yes,' I said, 'but how do we witches gain one familiar spirit, rather than another? Why do you stay with me?'

'Like draws to like,' she said, 'within the spirit realm, as in the earthly one. If the person's aims and objectives are the same as those of the familiar, and if friendship and respect are offered, then friendship will be given. Why would it not be?'

She went on to explain that, as well as spirit companions who may be with the witch for a lifetime or more, there are also brief relationships. This is because a familiar spirit may be drawn to help out a witch for a short period on a special project. Nature spirits, middle Earth contacts, will very much want to join forces with a witch who is working magically, or physically, to heal the land or protect the environment. Having been attracted by this deep concern, they may then help the witch in other ways, for instance with spells of healing for people, or with the wording of prayers or magical chants.

Faeries also very much want to heal the land, or rather, our relationship with it, but, as familiars, they tend to be drawn to those who like working with fate reading, prophecy and inspirational art – poetry, painting, song or dance, writing of any kind, or craftwork. They will certainly want us to use these arts to express the beauty and mystery of the land and so to inspire people to love mother nature and care for her.

Human discarnates may be people who knew us in earthly life, and therefore care for us. They may be dead friends or relations, or else they may be people who have ceased to reincarnate on this Earth, but who wish to help with the continuation of a certain kind of work. For example, they may have been witches themselves, or they may have been priests or priestesses of a Pagan tradition that they now wish to see reconstructed. They are called, in this instance, the ancestors, because they are our spiritual forebears. Both ancestors and faerie beings are underworld contacts.

There are no upperworld familiar spirits. Upperworld guidance is often received from one's own higher self, known in the Christian tradition as the guardian angel. This 'high elf' aspect of ourselves is our immortal spirit. The middle Earth aspect comprises our body, instincts and conscious personality. The underworld aspect is our soul, which, unlike the spirit, can be lost, damaged or destroyed, whereupon we lose hope, strength and individuality. Sadly, if we want to know what a person with a damaged or destroyed soul looks like, we only have to watch some of the passersby on any street.

High elves, who are not our own higher selves, but independent beings in their own right – the Shining Ones – are never familiar spirits to a witch or to anyone. This is because they oversee whole groups of people or aspects of life. We may meet with them psychically, but they do not stay with us to guide or assist us personally. It is a very special, very temporary contact, probably to do with some large issue. For instance, we may meet with the Shining Ones who oversee the Celtic race spirit or the art of peacemaking, but only if we can be instrumental in their concerns. This is because of the transpersonal nature of upperworld beings.

In spite of this, it is possible to meet psychically with, for example, a winged mermaid – one whose tail can transform into legs, so she can walk on land. Such a being undoubtedly has the freedom of all three realms, so we must be careful not to be overly rigid in our definition of the categories of spirits. Spiritual reality is not always arranged in three distinct layers, like a cake. In fact, the three realms overlap, and interpenetrate. But it is still true that our familiar spirits come from middle Earth or the underworld. These are the realms of our personal experiences and relationships.

To make sure that the upperworld aspect is very present in all work with our familiars, many witches place everything that we do under the protection of the Moon Goddess and/or Sun God (but equally, we could invoke a Sun Goddess or Moon God).

Just to make matters even more complicated, it is possible to have a familiar spirit who is a 'space' faerie. Traditionally, faeries have come to this Earth from other worlds – that is, from planets elsewhere in the Universe. They are especially linked with the Pleiades and with a star that used to circle the planet Sirius, and they may have come from other planets as well, to join the Earth faeries – and may still be coming. Such a space faerie may easily be a person's familiar spirit, if they wish it. However, this does not make them an upperworld contact. The upperworld is a state of consciousness and not a physical location. A space faerie is still an underworld being, whose work is soul weaving, wherever they originated. They are simply from the underworld dimension of some other planet, and that is all.

Of whichever type they are, familiar spirits give help that is invaluable. If you want to create magical prayers and rites but feel that you lack inspiration, then you need a familiar (well, we all need them for all kinds of reasons).

Sometimes, a beginner witch is afraid to attempt spirit communication, for fear of meeting with an evil one – and there are risks. There are disturbed, earth-bound human spirits in existence, nonhuman spirits of mischief, and ghouls.

Yet you are not going to be troubled by them, unless you ignore certain safety rules. For instance, it is obviously unwise to do any magical or psychic work in a place where bad things have been happening – like a haunted house, or a place where someone has experienced a severe breakdown, or where there has been violence or heavy drug use. This is because it is not wise to open your inner senses in a place where you may be exposed to a psychically toxic atmosphere, as this could make you feel depressed, disturbed or ill.

If you have just moved house, or if you feel that there is a bad atmosphere in your home for any reason, you can purify each room with a herb traditionally used for psychic cleansing. In Britain, these are pine and juniper, but frankincense is extremely effective, though nontraditional. In the Native American tradition, people use sage. You can vaporize essential oils of pine, juniper and frankincense, or any combination of these, and let the oil burner stand in each room in turn. Alternatively, you can burn any of them, including sage, as an incense, and carry it from room to room, filling your whole home with clouds of scented smoke.

The other safety rule is always to ask protection from the deities.

Now, as to methods of meeting with familiar spirits, the one I am about to suggest is very simple. If you want to try it then you must be in some quiet place, undisturbed. If indoors, light the candles on your altar. Say the following prayer to the Goddess, or something like it, for protection and psychic awareness.

Prayer to the Goddess for Psychic Protection and Sensitivity

Great Lady of the Moon and of visions and magic, I ask for your blessing. Surround me with your cloak

*of light, an aura of silver that no harm can penetrate.
And brighten my inner senses, all the knowing of the
night, that I may see or hear or sense the spirits.*

Now invoke the God, with the following prayer, or something
similar, so that you may ask him for the same assistance.

Prayer to the God for Psychic Protection and Awareness

*Horned God, I call to you, knowing you as master of
the old paths into forest or faerie. Within the dimensions where humans sleep, but the elementals and the
familiars move and affect the fate of mortals, you
guide and protect. Waken me to the true presence of
spirits. But keep me as safe as any wild creature who
knows you as Lord of Wisdom.*

If it is summer, you can have upon your altar a vase of valer-
ian, foxgloves, blackberry leaves, or any combination of these.
They are herbs that can increase contact with the faerie realms
and nature spirits. In winter, you might burn dried yarrow or
vervain, for psychic awareness. Alternatively, you can vaporize
the essential oils of bay or yarrow, or place willow leaves or, in
winter, place bare willow twigs, upon your altar.

This is the moment to offer up the flowers (if you have
them), ritually raising them above the altar, or to heap the
incense upon the charcoal or pour the essential oils into the
burner. Then say something like this.

Prayer to Meet with a Familiar Spirit

Great Lady and Lord of the spirit realms of Moon

and Wildwood, I ask you to send to me a familiar spirit. I ask to meet with one who will be in accord with my own best aspirations, and I with theirs. May she or he be kind, courageous, inspired, creative. May she or he be my lifelong companion, but only as the arrangement suits them as well as me. If I already have one such as this, may I know them clearly. If not, may a new link now be made, in love and wisdom.

Sit or lie down comfortably. Close your eyes. When you are ready, begin to visualize a big, beautiful, mysterious forest, or describe one to yourself. Take your time. See trunks of trees, see the branches and leaves, hear bird cries, see grass and wildflowers and winding pathways. Now the light begins to fade and the Moon rises. Follow a twisting path for a while, until you enter a glade. Stop here. This is the place.

Within the glade is a tall column of white light. It is magical, a round white tower. Within it, the three realms can meet or you can move between them. The tower is shining, as though made of clouds with the moonlight behind them, white, glowing. It is so tall, you can't see the top. Perhaps there isn't one. All around it is short green grass, the forest floor. Visualize that you're walking across this, right into the tower (it isn't solid, but like white mist, and you can walk through it easily). Inside is a circular space, about nine feet from side to side. The glowing white walls are now all around you, the grass still underneath your feet.

Say something like this.

In the names of the Lady of the Moon and the Lord of the Wildwood, I call to a familiar spirit. Come to me, you who seek a witch. Come to me, you who seek to assist with magic and to guide in wisdom. If I am, to you, a suitable pupil, or good companion upon the

*path, if you are of my path, come to me now. I pledge
myself to hear your counsel and to share my life and
powers and possibilities, as it harms none.*

You may want to alter this wording to include your special
interests. For example, you might say, *Come to me, you
who seek to assist with healing.* You may mention artwork
or ritual, wildlife or music, or, of course, prayer. But you do
not need to be too specific, unless you want to. Your call will
go out far and wide – a sort of psychic advertisement!
Familiars drawn to you will come because they can sense
your real interests or read them in your aura.

See the white walls swirl toward you, thickening up so you
can't see a hand in front of your face. All is white mist. Then
the clouds shift and clear – and you are in a different landscape. This may be a seashore, another wood, the inside of
a hollow hill where there is a faerie court, anything. The first
being that you see coming toward you should be your familiar. Ask them if that is what they are. They may nod or in
some other way signify assent, and then speak to you, telepathically, inside your mind.

If you already have a familiar spirit and have known it for
some while, then the psychic atmosphere of this spirit will be
– familiar. You are used to one another's presence. But this
may be the very first proper meeting, so you will now have a
chance to expand and deepen the whole relationship.

As I have said, the familiar could be any kind of creature,
or a faerie or a discarnate human. Some people even report
that they have a familiar that seems quite abstract. A shape
of light or something elemental, like a fire spirit. So long as
you feel comfortable with what you see, anything is all right.
This is your familiar spirit, and your business.

After you have seen your familiar – or sensed them if you
do not have the Sight – ask for their name. The first word
you hear, within your mind, will be it. You may use this name

to call to your familiar from now on, repeating it three times, when you are seeking assistance with the writing of a prayer or designing of a spell, or when you need psychic protection, healing or guidance. If you see them but do not immediately hear a name, you may call them by describing what you saw, e.g. fox, woman in green, spirit of the forest, jackdaw, otter, faerie priest, etc.

Ask them to strengthen the link between you, and to open your psychic senses, so that you can see or hear or sense them more strongly. Thank them for coming to meet you, and tell them that you hope to work with them, in a strong and creative magical partnership, from now on.

Next, ask if there is anything they would like you to do, to strengthen the connection between the two of you. You may sense or hear the reply or they may show you a symbol of some kind. It may or may not seem rational. For instance, you may be asked to collect fallen feathers of a particular species of bird, and keep them on your altar, or to visit a certain place, or to use a specific essential oil or incense – or anything at all. These answers may have something to do with attuning you to the familiar's own nature, like visiting lakes and rivers if you have a moorhen, otter or swan familiar, for example. They may be for strengthening your psychic awareness – for instance, the changing of your diet or lifestyle. Whatever you feel you are being asked to do, so long as it is harmless, you have nothing to lose and very much to gain by doing it.

Continue the conversation for as long as you want to, before bidding them 'Hail and farewell', with thanks and with promises to meet again. Now ask them to protect your inner senses, restoring your entire psyche to a suitable state for the mundane world. Visualize a protective symbol (like a pentagram or equal-armed cross within a circle) above your head. And open your eyes.

From now on, you may call to your familiar spirit whenever you need to. Always end any communication by asking them to prepare your senses and your soul for the everyday world – and visualizing your protective symbol.

As I have said before, not everyone is clairvoyant. If you find even visualization to be impossible, then do not worry. Just say the prayers and then describe the wood and the tower of light to yourself, inside your mind. When you get to the bit where you call out to a familiar, stop and read or say it out loud, in a ritual manner. Then sit quietly and see what you can sense in the psychic atmosphere around you. Begin to talk, inside your mind, to any presence that may be there, whether you can feel them or not. Request them to open your psychic senses – but gently and very safely – or to announce their presence in some way, or appear to you in a dream. Then thank them and ask them for psychic protection, as you end the session.

Now, as to the subject of whether we can actually talk to a bird or animal or faerie being – or to a discarnate Pictish priest – since none of these speak our own language, it would appear there are huge difficulties. The answer is simple. They do not speak to us, but convey the essence of ideas, information and so on, telepathically. It is our own minds that supply the language, translating what we have understood into our own vocabulary. Psychic communication is essentially nonverbal, but we need words if we are to grasp concepts consciously enough to act upon them and to understand – so we supply the words ourselves.

Some people might object, saying that they cannot see how a bird, or horse or any animal spirit could have a developed enough consciousness to help us. 'Surely', such people would say, 'the creatures are limited in their perceptions. Even as spirits they cannot understand what health advice we might need, nor the practice of magic, nor the web of fate. Nor even our feelings.' Are we sure about that?

The question remains open as to whether the spirit friends

we meet are, objectively, separate beings from ourselves, or aspects of our own minds, personified as a faerie, dog, thrush, eagle, wisewoman, or whatever else. One day we will know. Meanwhile, if our familiars can give good advice, accurate predictions about the future, a tangible increase in energy when we are tired and assistance with magical prayers and spells (or at least some of these), then it may not be useful to analyze them too far. Our culture has a strong need to dissect and label, often from a rather mechanistic viewpoint. Sometimes this is good, but over the issue of who or what our spirit friends are, it may be pointlessly destructive.

I believe my own familiars to be quite separate from myself. It is not that cut off, unrecognized aspects of ourselves do not exist. Indeed they do, as certain modern schools of thought, like psychosynthesis, have stated clearly. But ancient Pagan belief, as expressed in shamanistic cultures, has always recognized the difference between a part of one's own soul that has been traumatized and suppressed (soul retrieval then being necessary), and the spirit friends who help with such work.

Any witch or Pagan mystic can acquire real familiars to guide or help her or him. Even if you cannot immediately see, hear or sense the spirit you have called to, be assured that they are there.

The easiest way to talk with a familiar is to write a dialogue with them. This is especially useful for getting their input on prayers, spells or plans for rituals. Sit quietly in some peaceful place with a notebook and pen. Write a formal request for their presence – something like this: *Hail, familiar spirit* [or call them by name]. *I ask you to be here and talk with me. I ask for guidance.*

Now, switch your pen to your other hand, the one you don't usually write with, to jot down their replies. Switch back to your normal writing hand to write your own next part of the dialogue – and so on. In this way, you can have a really long conversation, and even take down prayers and entire rituals at their dictation.

In time, it becomes easier to write with your other hand. You may never become as fluent or legible as with your dominant hand, but you do get better at it. The nondominant hand is said to be linked, via the nervous system, with the more intuitive hemisphere of the brain. This is why it seems easier to use, when in psychic communication. Whatever the rationale, it works very well, but you do have to practice until you get used to it.

As with trance conversation, the first thing that you hear inside your mind will be your familiar spirit's answer. If it doesn't make sense at first, don't worry. Just write it down anyway. As you continue the conversation, it will become clearer.

What should you do if something horrible, frightening or insane is dictated to you? Stop – and call upon the Goddess and God to banish this intrusive spirit. Then call upon your real familiar and ask her/him to protect you. Then visualize your protective symbol. Go and do something other than psychic work for a while, until your psyche recovers from this disturbance. I think it very unlikely that you will find this sort of thing happens to you. In fifteen years of guided writing, I have never known it to occur. In theory, it could do, and the above is what I would advise in that event – but it would be rare.

Of course, you should never act upon advice from a familiar if it seems unbalanced, unwise or likely to lead to some danger. Needless to say, bad advice will not be from a real familiar, but from a spirit intruder or from some unconscious, angry part of your own mind. Use common sense to decide what is good, genuine advice and what is not – the same rule that would apply if you were being advised by someone in the ordinary, everyday world.

In any case, even if the advice sounds as if it could be right, you do not have to act upon it. It is never right to give up our autonomy to another being, not even to a wise familiar spirit. They are not there to demand our slavish obedience, any more than we should impose that upon them. The relationship of master/mistress and slave, or even of guru and disciple, is not recommended to a witch or a wildwood mystic. Not even within the inner realms.

Some people fear that they will start hearing lots of 'little voices' through doing this work. This is not so. The familiar's voice stops the minute you put down the pen, and bid them 'Hail and farewell, with thanks'. It is a discipline, a technique. Safety rules have been included here, but in fact, there is more danger in being deaf to all spirit voices, as so many people are in today's world.

13 Traveling Between the Worlds

Our shamanistic forebears, the tribal 'ancestors' of every witch, traveled up and down the world tree, or between the three levels, in the course of their healing work. There are several traditional methods by which such travel can be undertaken, and I will describe one.

Naturally, such journeys are made in our spirits. There is little point in attempting to reach the upperworld by standing on a hilltop, unless we grow wings inside ourselves! The three realms are states of being – or of consciousness – rather than physical locations. Having said that, it is easier to reach the underworld psychically, when you are actually on a beach, in a cave or by a holy well – or to talk with middle Earth's nature spirits in a beautiful garden or in a wood – or to commune with Shining Ones of the upperworld on hills or mountains. As for stone circles or other sacred sites, these are often places where the spirits and deities of any realm can be met with easily, which is why people go to them. When wishing to travel 'between the worlds', whether at home or at a chosen place of pilgrimage, prayers can be said to begin the process. You can say something like this.

Prayer to Travel Between the Worlds

Great Goddess and God of all Realms of Existence, here in this sacred place, I invoke you. I ask that the

*veils be parted, allowing me to enter the land of spirit
and to travel freely between the worlds.*

Now sit or lie comfortably, with your eyes closed. You can
then say, *May the spirits of middle Earth/the underworld/
the upperworld hear me now and draw near. I approach
your realm seeking guidance/healing/assistance. I ask for
safe passage.*

Now imagine that you are sitting or lying beneath a tall
tree. This may be a silver birch, or a splendid oak, or an ash
or apple, or, indeed, any tree which feels right to you.

Call to your familiar spirit and ask them to meet you here,
beside the tree. When he or she has arrived or you can hear
their voice, explain to them what you want to achieve now,
and ask them to show you how to travel to the right realm.
A number of things may then happen. Remember, you will
be seeing all this in your 'mind's eye' like an extra bright
daydream, if you have the Sight. If not, simply say the prayer
and remind yourself of the world tree and then, inwardly, ask
your familiar spirit to take you to the upperworld, middle
Earth or the underworld. Trust that it is happening and see if
you can sense any change in the atmosphere around you. If
you do this kind of thing often enough, you will begin to
develop the Sight anyway.

If it is the upperworld you wish to reach, your familiar may
then lead you, in your mind's eye, to a nearby hill. Upon the
summit, there waits a magnificent, winged, white horse.
Visualize all these things as clearly as you can. Staring in awe,
you begin to realize why our ancestors carved white chalk
horses upon hillsides in southern Britain. This creature is the
land personified, and something more. It is the transcendent
beauty of the land's spirit, implying (paradoxically) other
worlds, other ways. Mount the horse with your familiar, or
ask them to travel alongside, and you will then be taken up,
flying high up in the sky. You pass through clouds and then

clear blue height, miles and miles of it. Finally, leaving the Earth's atmosphere, you enter space. Planets and stars rush along past you, for the horse goes at the speed of thought.

You ask to be taken to the place where you most need to be, for the guidance that you seek, or the healing for yourself or for another. Landing upon the Moon or Sun, or upon a star or another planet, you find not a barren place or ball of burning gas, but a golden or silver sea of light. Gradually, this clears and you find yourself in a lovely landscape. . . . As you ride along through it, observe what is around you. Eventually, the horse stops and it is here that you must dismount. What is the place like? What do you see? There comes toward you an upperworld spirit, one of the tall Shining Ones, who appear as large beings made entirely of light. They may be winged, or they may not, but they are always very beautiful as presences (though their features may be concealed from you, veiled in light). Ask for a blessing, and for advice about any healing which is required. You may be shown an object or a creature of some kind. This will be important in the healing you seek, for yourself or a friend, for its particular upperworld symbolism.

To take a simple example, you may be shown a rose. Its upperworld, ideal or spiritual meaning, as most people know, is love. The message would be that love is the power of healing that is most needed. But if you had been shown this symbol in middle Earth, then it could have meant that the physical properties of the rose were wanted, as an aromatherapy oil or an incense. If you had been shown it in the underworld, the faeries could have said that an actual romance, as opposed to a generalized spiritual love for all beings, was what you needed – or were about to have!

If shown a symbol which you do not understand, ask to be shown or told more, until you understand better. In the end, simply take what is offered, and thank the high elf for giving it.

Ask any more questions that spring to mind. If you do not hear or see the answers at once, remember they may come to you when you least expect it (following a spirit journey like this, the right inspiration can come when you're cleaning your teeth, or waiting for a bus). At times, you may be taken, by a Shining One, to meet other beings or to have further adventures. When all is complete, thank them for the meeting. Get back on the horse and ask to be taken home. Once again, you will rise up and fly through space, then descend through the Earth's atmosphere, to land on the hilltop. Thank the horse and walk back to the tree, with your familiar spirit. Ask her or him to put a sphere of silver light around you, as psychic protection upon your return to the mundane world. And open your eyes.

As I said, it is still perfectly possible to do this work, even if your mind's eye stays firmly shut. You can talk yourself through the stages of it, describing them in your mind. At the crux of the story, you say to yourself something like, 'Now I meet with a Shining One. This is a being of great purity and wisdom. I ask the following questions. "What is the healing most needed by myself/my friend? What form could this healing take?" They put the answers into my mind – where I shall be able to perceive them in a dream or as a sudden realization in my daily life.' All you have to do then is to trust that this will happen.

If you talk yourself through a trance journey, like the one above, you may find it changes. The story may start to develop in unexpected ways. It may go off, seemingly at a tangent, to describe a rather more complex adventure. If this happens, it is a very good sign! It means that your psychism is developing as clairaudience (what you hear with your 'mind's ear') rather than as clairvoyance. Do not strive to make this happen. To do so actually blocks it, because you become tense. Just be relaxed and let things happen naturally.

If you are shown, or hear of, an unpleasant symbol when you have asked about healing, this may mean that health will ensue on getting rid of what is causing an illness. For example, when talking with middle Earth spirits, you may be shown what looks like a lot of black mould. This could mean, 'your house is damp and this is undermining your health'.

It is not always easy to interpret symbols when we are fraught with anxiety about the possible meaning. Sometimes, a familiar spirit can explain it for us. At other times, it is best to keep an open mind, while exploring various options for remedial action. We can also ask 'What would be the best means of banishing or dealing with this cause of illness?' and should then be shown a more positive symbol.

The same kind of work can be done if you want to journey in middle Earth or in the underworld. To be in middle Earth, stand under the world tree and imagine that you call to the horse to meet you there. Then mount and go for a ride across open country. After a while, you are taken to (or visualize) an immense forest. Entering it, you travel along paths until you reach a green glade where you can speak with nature spirits. These may be the spirits of trees, or you may talk to a fox, badger or bird, or many different creatures. As with the upperworld, if you visit this place enough, your adventures will change. You may be taken from the forest to somewhere quite unexpected. You may see scenes out of history. All this will have a symbolic meaning, or a psychic one. For example, if seeing historical events in middle Earth, you may be being advised that your home or workplace is haunted. Alternatively, you may be watching a scenario which describes certain psychological pressures or political worries, in your own or your friend's mind. If in doubt, ask your familiar spirit for an explanation, and ask to be advised of the right remedy. In fact, you should always ask your familiar spirit for advice or psychic assistance if you are stuck, confused, overwhelmed or in any way disturbed or disempowered.

When you are shown some physical treatment for an illness, like a particular herb, it is best to seek the advice of a qualified herbalist for confirmation, and to be told if it should be in tablet or tincture form, and in what dosage. Of course, this does not apply if the guidance has been very simple, like 'Drink more peppermint tea'.

Herbs of all kinds can be an important aspect of magical work, whether as incenses, medicine, essential oils or in other ways. But, unless we are medical herbalists, it is right to use them only as first aid treatments – or else magically, rather than medically – without ingesting them. For example, you could be shown a sprig from a yew tree, and advised that it is a healing remedy. Yew, as most of us know, is poisonous, and any attempt to make a herbal tea from it would be quite insane. However, as a magical substance, it means regeneration and immortality (which is why our Pagan ancestors often planted yew at burial places, a tradition carried on by the Christians. Physically, biologically, the yew has a miraculous, phoenixlike ability to resurrect itself when apparently dead. Small slips of it can therefore be used in a spell to regenerate someone's artistic inspiration, to bring back hope for someone in despair or to make a new start when someone has lost what they most valued e.g. a relationship, loved home or fulfilling job. This can be done very simply by placing the evergreen yew twigs in a vase, to be left in the room where they sleep. These should be consecrated to the regeneration of the named person, as a link between them and the living energy of yew trees, in their aspect of rebirth.

This kind of work, done magically with the essences and spirits of natural objects or plants or creatures, is what witches and our forebears, the tribal healers, have always done. It is a skill that develops with practice and is based in wildwood mysticism. Although it can be done very easily, as with spells like the one I have just described, it is also a lifetime's study – or many lifetimes.

To travel to the underworld, you may ask the horse to take you down into a cave. At the back of it, there is a passageway, along which you ride deeper into the Earth. Down winding tunnels the horse walks, the route lit only by candles that are set into niches along the rock walls. At the bottom of the slope, there is a wide underground river. The horse wades across it. On the far side, you are in a faerie landscape. There is no longer a rock roof above you, just open sky. You can see apple trees that are in fruit, leaf and blossom all at once. The horse may lead you to a lake within the faerie realm. In the middle of it, there is an island. Dismount from the horse, for a boatman waits for you. When he has ferried you across, you will meet faerie beings upon the lake shores or amongst the trees. These may not be people. You may meet a faerie wild cat, or a hound or blackbird or, indeed, anything. Ask the first creature you see to take you to the faerie queen or one of her representatives. You may then enter a walled garden. It is abundant with wild roses, rowan trees, blackberries, all kinds of wildflowers and there are more apple trees. This garden also has a sacred well from which, if you drink, you will be purified of something that is obstructing your development as a person, or as a witch. You will be purified at whatever cost (in terms of how your life will then change), so do not drink unless you are prepared for this.

After a while, you will see somebody coming toward you. It may not be she whom you have asked to see, for she may not judge that you are ready; but someone will come, faerie woman or man, who can help you. Ask any question you want to ask. This may concern health, changes in the pattern of fate, techniques for magic, or whatever is important to you at the time.

It is often good to ask for a blessing from any faerie creature or person whom you may meet, as you would with the nature spirits or Shining Ones. All are messengers of the Great Goddess or God, they are their representatives, as are we, ourselves, in our most profound, creative or divine aspect. You may also want to give blessings, as this is always a kindly act.

When you are ready, give thanks and return to the boatman. On reaching the shore where the horse waits, mount and ask to return to middle Earth. You will then recross the river, go back up the rock passageway and emerge from the cave. On reaching the world tree, dismount and thank the horse. Then ask your familiar to put the silver protective sphere round you, so that you may not be too disturbed by harsh atmospheres in the everyday world. You should, of course, also ask for protection after returning from the forest on your middle Earth journey, but I think that I forgot to say so.

If you get stuck on a trance journey – that is, if you cannot shift into altered consciousness nor make any headway – always resort to prayer. Call upon the Goddess and God of whichever realm you are trying to enter, and ask them to help you. It is also always worth asking your familiar spirit to open your psychic senses, and to transmit to you the psychic energy you require to achieve your goal. These things almost always work. If they do not, it may mean you are just simply too tired, since psychic work can be exhausting when we are already low on energy. It can also be revitalizing but, as with physical exercise, this only helps if there is something to draw upon in the first place. Whatever the reason, if it's not working out, pray to be shown the right time and place for a trance journey later. And, as always, end with a request to your familiar spirit for a sphere of protection. Many people would actually recommend that you begin inner work by asking for the silver sphere. Ideally, you should, but somehow I never seem to remember to do that myself. I suppose that is because I feel safer in Pagan spirit realms than in the human world! In the event of meeting some unpleasant and destructive spirit (and this can happen, partly because there are astral entities created by human psychic activity), I always ask my familiar spirit to remove it. I instruct them to take it to a place where it will be transformed, until it is in harmony with the Lady and Lord, and with all creation. This always works.

I hope that this chapter has given some kind of glimpse of the fabulous possibilities for psychic experience available to a wildwood mystic. These practices will not unfold for you immediately, unless you have had previous psychic experience. But if you persevere, in a relaxed way, in a spirit of adventure, then I promise you will have results. By combining prayer and visualization (or by telling yourself the story), and with the help of your familiar spirit, you can part the veils inside yourself. Thus you enter realms where encounters with faeries, nature spirits and Shining Ones can be experienced. These encounters are real, they are not merely meetings with aspects of your own self. You will be able to know this. It is a matter of experience.

We are all learning. No one can claim to know everything there is to know about the three realms, which are infinite, nor always to get it right – not unless they have achieved ultimate wisdom. But, on the winged horse, we can travel hopefully.

Other methods of moving between the realms include visualizing that you are flying on a broomstick, or moving upstairs or downstairs inside a crystal tower. In time, you may discover which works best for you.

Start with just one journey in whichever realm most appeals (though, in time, you may travel freely between them all in one session). Keep it brief and simple for a first attempt and do not worry if the results seem undramatic. These things only develop with practice. You would not expect to play a concerto the first time you picked up a flute. If you never 'see' anything, just describe events inside your own mind, intuitively following twists in the plot until you know that you can hear spirit voices. Once they begin to give accurate predictions and useful advice, you will know that it has ceased to be 'just' your own imagination.

14   Steps Along the Path

The shape of the wildwood mystic's path is not like that of a straight track, from a to b, in a linear progression. It is more of a spiral from a to *be*, on which we travel between the three realms. I cannot draw this symbol as a diagram, because it is not a straightforward winding up and down. The shape is more like that of a spiraling labyrinth, twisting and turning one way and then another, moving us toward the heart of one or other of the three realms – and then back out again.

There is an ancient glyph, the triple spiral, in which three flat spiral shapes are connected from a central point. It looks something like this.

Poppy Palin

This is a simplification, in which our labyrinthine spiral in and out of three realms is encapsulated.

Another symbol for us to meditate upon is that of the famous 'Cretan' labyrinth – which shape is found carved on rock faces or standing stones from Greece to Britain to North America.

The labyrinth's meaning is that turning inward, to the underworld or upperworld, or the psychic dimension of middle Earth, is always followed by a return to the outer or everyday world, bearing the spiritual insights or psychic gifts which we have gained. This works in exactly the same way that sitting down to mull things over is followed by a decisive action. Therefore, the symbol describes a natural process which we have all experienced, in one form or another.

The point is that each time we go within, we are transformed, however slightly. We will have learned something and also been in communion with spirit, which will have altered our innermost being. The goal is to come into harmony within ourselves, with one another and with all life. The means by which we hope (however many lives it takes) to achieve this, is the development of wisdom. We journey in quest of that. The path is a labyrinthine spiral that stands up, vertically (luckily, we do not need to visualize that to be walking it!).

To a witch, the process of turning within is symbolized as an anticlockwise movement, called going 'widdershins' or 'moonwise'. We can dance or twirl or circle widdershins, to help bring about the altered consciousness needed for inner work. On such a journey within, we may encounter obstacles like our own fears or prejudices, society's phobias in the form of our conditioning, or various spirits, who test and challenge us. On arriving at the centre, some knowledge is gained, some monster faced out and/or some new magical ability attained. We then return (clockwise or deosil, as it is symbolized) into outer consciousness, stronger and richer in insight, more able to be creative with magic and in all ways.

In formal ritual, the widdershins dance or walk is often used to banish something, and the deosil (clockwise) dance to build power. Upon the wildwood mystic's path, what we are banishing, when we turn widdershins, are the worldly distractions that prevent psychic communion with spirit realms. What we are aiming to build, on our deosil return, is a creative life, a wiser self, and a more harmonious world.

Deliberately undertaken spirit journeys are not the whole story. These open the three realms for us, in terms of understanding, and give us magical insights and assistance, as described in the previous chapter. But also, they mimic a much larger and more long-term process which is happening for us all, whether consciously using spiritual practices, or not. Wildwood mysticism is, after all, about natural spirituality, that which is simply endemic to everyone's existence, and not optional. We all, whether witches or not, descend to the underworld at certain times in our lives, and in our dreams. Within this place, we struggle with our inner selves. Psychological tangles and distorted emotions must all be processed or healed in the underworld, however long it takes. As well as that, our souls gain in psychic richness down in the depths. It is here that we learn to respond to art and poetry, to be capable of passionate love and to experience the mystery of a birth or bereavement, as well as the risk or pain.

Sometimes, we can get stuck, uncomfortably, in the depths. Mental illnesses and depression can spring from avoiding the proffered insights and from confusion about which way to turn, to reach the centre (or the bottom) where the healing wisdom lies. I am sure we can all remember times when we have been stuck like this for long months or even years. That does not make it a bad place. In fact, I am tempted to say it is the most important of the three, or the one in which the most crucial work must be done, anyway.

To go back to our image of the tree, the world tree, if the roots were not healthy, the trunk, leaves and branches (all creation) would be doomed. The same goes for each one of us, as individual 'trees'. We cannot live creative, wise, environmentally sound lives unless, psychologically, we are reasonably healthy. We cannot get a full sense of life's meaning and sacredness unless we are faerie led into the realms of creative play, stories, make-believe and magic. Any child knows this but, as adults, we can forget. It is part of a witch's job to remember it, for the world's sake.

When we spiral inward in middle Earth, we are learning the sacredness of nature, the presence of nature spirits, the holiness of the body, the consciousness-expanding properties of sexuality and many other wonderful things. Here, through contact with plants and creatures and elements, we gain much healing. Friendship with animals, talking to plants, daydreaming in woodland glades, and other similar often mocked but valuable activities, are all a part of this process. Our struggle, as we turn outward back into the world, is how to integrate an awareness of nature's wisdom with our physical survival, our practicality. It may not be going too far to say that if, as a culture, we do not achieve this middle Earth initiation, we will not survive. It means living wisely and kindly upon the Earth, creatively, with respect for all species. The keyword here is 'environmentalism', based in our actual spiritual experiences of being at one with all life, a child of Mother Earth. This is one reason that Paganism is currently what the world most needs to hear about.

In the upperworld, we turn within for our inspiration, in terms of ideals: the vision of the ideal life, and ideal world; the principles that we live by; transcendence of our own personal worries or desires, for the sake of our beliefs or the common good. The world's mainstream or dominant religions have tended to focus most strongly on upperworld concerns, aiming straight for the top. This has meant relegating the realms of middle Earth and the underworld to an alleged dimension of evil – because both sensuality and magic dwell there, and because the underworld's buried truths may be subversive to any hierarchical organization. My second book *Lamp of the Goddess* deals in some depth with these issues.

At present, we have a culture in which fixed and rigid ideologies too often take the place of visions that genuinely serve the common good. Aiming for the heights of academic qualification or successful commercial output can override true inspiration. We do not look at nor value the Earth that we are standing on, except as material to be exploited. We do not honor our deeply held feelings, nor the magic inherent in life, because we have been taught to regard these as sinister and dangerous. But, as the briefest glance round our world indicates, it is a mistake to go to the upperworld until we have explored both middle Earth and the underworld thoroughly.

This point is recognized in organized Wicca. Within witches' covens, there are three grades or initiations, available to all. The first degree initiation is that of middle Earth. Here, the neophyte witch learns something of nature's wisdom and sacredness, comes to understand the cycle of seasons and the Moon's phases, and also acquires some practical skills, like the making of incenses, wands and so on. She or he must also know something of the magical symbolism of plants and creatures. The development of some magical crafts – hands-on activities like the building of fires, the sewing of ritual robes and the making of bread or wine – might also be expected. This initiation is taken successfully when we understand that all objects and creatures and places – all beings – are spirit in a manifest form.

The second degree initiation is that of the underworld. The witch of this grade understands inner demons within the psyche, has met with faeries, can read the future and knows – or should – at least something about how to heal psychic pain, create a good psychic atmosphere, tell a healing story or create magical artwork. Strictly speaking, we cannot attain this grade without having faced inner truths – the truth of our own soul.

Third degree witches, the high priestesses or priests, understand – or should – about the connection between our personal magic and universal forces. They see the large picture, aware that sex magic and group dynamics cannot only be harnessed to serve the common good and the land, but also to make connections of many kinds between the divine and the mundane.

We are all, whether in covens or not, taking and retaking various forms of these three initiations continually, throughout all our lives – whether witches of any kind or not, and whether we know it or not. Each time we take each one we learn something new, and take it on a different arc of our understanding. The point, in the end, is to achieve wisdom, that we might all live in creative harmony with one another and all beings.

As wildwood mystics, whether we are witches or any other type of Pagan magical practitioner, we work consciously with this process. We do this in order to gain understanding and wisdom more easily and swiftly, and to access psychic dimensions for magic and healing. But we should be under no illusion that the three realms are specially ours, because we do magic – they are everybody's, all beings are within them. What is ours, especially, is knowledge of them; not just as theory, but as experience.

If all this seems too complicated, don't worry. For one thing, it is in the nature of mystery to defy attempts to explain it. So I'll repeat, because it's important: wildwood mysticism is what we experience, rather than what we conceptualize, within the psychic dimensions of the world tree. It is a living thing – unwieldy, fertile, paradoxical, exciting, puzzling. It is mysterious.

So what do we actually do on this path? What are our disciplines and techniques. After all that theory, I think I should summarize the practices of a wildwood mystic, as outlined in this book. Where does the path begin and how do we keep on treading it? Well, of course it begins at a tree. Here is a list of nine steps on the path. Once you have taken those, you will be shown what the next ones are by your familiars.

1   Initiation on the path of the wildwood mystic, using the ritual described in chapter five, or something similar.

2   The building of a wildwood altar within your home. This need not be exactly as described. In fact, it is better if your own creativity and interests are represented. However all three realms around the world tree should be shown, in some form. The simple vase of twigs to symbolize the entire tree is a good start.

3   Design a Pagan prayer routine that can be used daily. If this seems daunting, just start with one-liners, such as, *Great Goddess, let me be true to your purposes and so to my innermost self*, or *Great God, please guide me to magical knowledge*. If short prayers like this are all that you can say, then perhaps they are all that you need, for the time being. Keep the commitment to saying them and they will blossom or transform, eventually.

4   Take the initiation of the hedge witch, so that your mysticism may be dedicated to the service of life, through magical practices designed to heal and assist others and yourself. Use the ritual in chapter seven, or something similar. Or, if you prefer a more formal rite, use the one from the book *The Wiccan Path*, or something of that kind.

147

5   Meet with your familiar spirit(s), as described in chapter twelve. With their help, begin to go upon inner journeys, as described in chapter thirteen. Here is where you will gain magical insights that transform and strengthen you. Here, also, you will gain assistance with healing magic.

6   Go upon pilgrimages in the outer world, too, as often as you can. Visit wild places. A wildwood mystic is not confined to a town or city, even if living there. She or he should make the most of any wild places that can be found in the town, or any holy wells or sites of beauty.

When it comes to places exemplifying the mysteries of middle Earth, you can visit local woodlands, public gardens, riverbanks or hills. Say prayers there for healing, guidance and insight.

As for the underworld, have you ever been to a magical island? There are many of them: Iona, Lewes – the whole of the Hebrides, really – the Orkneys, Lindisfarne, the Scillies, Lundy, Caldey Island and Anglesey, to name a few. Where are your local ones, whether you live in Britain or not? Are there any lake islands close to you? Have you ever been on a boat to an island, as a deliberate Pagan pilgrimage? When you go to such a place, you can pray that the veils will be parted for you, so that you gain entry to the otherworldly dimension, and so that you may receive guidance and healing from the island's faerie folk. Then explore the place and see what happens.

Caves are a rather more obvious approach to the underworld. Near where I live there are famous ones – Cheddar and Wookey Hole. Of course, the tour guides do babble away constantly, as you go through with them. Sometimes their spiel is in bad taste and quite irritating. Nevertheless, places like Wookey Hole are fantastically potent for the Pagan mystic. The river Axe, which flows through these caves, is a British equivalent of the Greek river Styx. To cross it, by the narrow bridge that exists there, is a very profound experience – or can be. Prayers can be said for an inner purification or psychic transformation of ourselves, so that the crossing is a dedicated act, a ritual. For example, you can say, *As I cross the river, may I move from death to life, my psychic senses cleansed and reborn.* Indeed, such a crossing can be dedicated to many aims e.g. connection with the realm of spirits, increased psychological understanding, a better knowledge of fate, a new way of life that is more magical. Needless to say, any river or stream can be used as a substitute for the river Axe, if you do not live near to Somerset. At the source, each of them rises from underground.

Then there is the upperworld. Have you ever been to the London Planetarium? Looked through a powerful telescope at the stars and planets? Or, most importantly of all, stood somewhere out in the country and looked at the night sky? To do so within a stone circle can be especially wonderful. You can ask to be shown the connection between the stars and Moon (or Sun) and our Earth. After all, that is the main reason for which stone circles are believed to have been built – to celebrate and to amplify the physical, and the subtle or spiritual, aspects of these relationships, which create obvious cycles like the year and the month, and other less obvious ones, too. Having asked, you may see visions, or simply feel the links, the power of the stars upon Earth.

7   With the help of familiar spirits, and as a result of your mystical experiences, begin to cast spells for all kinds of creative and healing purposes. If in doubt as to how to construct a spell, ask to receive guidance. Write down the ideas that familiar spirits have suggested, plus any information gained in your trance journeying. Proceed from there.

8 Ground wildwood mysticism in your daily life. This may mean unglamorous tasks, like picking up litter on a local beach or clearing out lager cans from a spring or woodland pool. It will undoubtedly mean honoring the natural, and nature's laws, in how we dress, what we eat, what we do with our time, how we treat our illnesses, what we teach our children. As wildwood mystics, it is the nature spirits who help and heal and instruct us – and the faeries, whose home is the realm of nature's deep soul – so our lives reflect this, by the offerings we make to nature.

9 Begin to link many magical intentions with your creative tasks. As already stated in earlier chapters, you can dedicate many activities, like sewing, dancing, poetry, making love, cookery, gardening, making music or writing, to magic. In time-honored fashion, this is what has always been done in traditional witchcraft. Crooning a magical charm over sewing or weaving is an ancient practice. Poetry easily becomes enchantment – the rhythmic use of words for spellcraft. The witch's cauldron is just a cooking pot, really. Shamanic healers and witches have always danced ritually, and so on. From doll making to candle making to herb teas (magical potions), witches have always used arts and crafts to express and to work magic. Ask your familiar spirits for guidance about the best ways to use your own talents or develop new ones.

These nine steps outline the practices of any wildwood mystic and hedge witch. They can be done in ways that are quite formal, utilizing the discipline of a full magic circle as described in many books on the Craft, or they can be done informally, as described in this book. All witches develop their own distinctive style. What works for you? This becomes clear when you are experienced.

Wherever you are in your life process – on the underworld quest for deep healing, enjoying inspiration from upperworld sources, or engaged in bringing up children or building some project that is creative in middle Earth – you can still visit the spirit dimensions of any of the three realms (or all of them) at any time, and so assist yourself and others. Which one do you feel at home in? I believe most witches are underworld creatures by nature, with one foot in fairyland. But remember, the world tree is three in one. The Great Goddess and the God are triple but are one. The three realms interrelate, and there is no sharp line dividing them, nor limiting their work: starlight shines on the sea, the underground spring flows out into middle Earth, and some of the faeries who live in the hollow hills can fly.

The mystery is three in one and points to integration – a potential alignment within ourselves of divine inspiration with natural creativity and profound magic, or of spirit, body and soul. This is the fabulous and ideal theme within Paganism, the treasure we look for.

15 Prayers for the Eight Sabbats

Everyone knows that witches have sabbats. These are the sacred days, or festivals, that witches celebrate. Those who work in covens meet up with their fellow witches on these days, and enact the rites that are appropriate to the time. These may take place out of doors at a sacred site, especially in the summer. For hedge witches, also, the festivals may be an occasion for pilgrimage, either alone or with a magical partner or friends. We may visit a well or a particular tree. We may climb a hill or walk by a river or by the sea. These excursions are a personal celebration of any sacred day, and a chance to be at one with the tides of magic, which flow strongly in nature at the festivals. Rites may be enacted while at the site of pilgrimage, consisting of prayers and consecrated acts, like drinking water from a well or dancing around in a circle of standing stones. The witch will return home renewed, sometimes to work further magic, on a formal or informal basis, at her or his altar.

On the eve of a sabbat, it is right that the altar should be prepared. Dust it, remove caked-on candle wax and wash or dust all the ritual objects that you keep there. Then fill a small vase with flowers and also decorate the altar with anything that is seasonal e.g. holly, ivy and mistletoe at Yule, eggs at the spring equinox etc.

The word 'sabbat', as used by witches, refers to any one of the eight annual festivals celebrated in Britain by our Celtic and Saxon ancestors, and also by the pre-Celtic people who built our stone circles. Each of the sabbats celebrates either a beginning or a midpoint of one of the four seasons. They do this by marking phases in the relationship between the Sun and the Earth – from which the seasons, of course, originate. Two of the sabbats are the winter and summer solstices. There are also the equinoxes, which occur in spring and autumn. The solstices and equinoxes are called the lesser sabbats. The midpoints, between each equinox and the next solstice, known as Beltane, Lughnasadh, Samhain and Imbolg, are called the greater sabbats. In fact, each of the greater sabbats begins a season: Beltane, on May Eve, marks the start of summer; Lughnasadh, 1 August, begins autumn; Samhain, 31 October, is winter's beginning; and Imbolg, 2 February, is the start of spring. The solstices and equinoxes are culminations – and also changing points. Midsummer is celebrated at the summer solstice, whilst the winter solstice marks the turning point of midwinter. Likewise, equinoxes show changing tides within spring and autumn.

In brief, each sabbat is a day on which a particular type of seasonal energy runs high. That tide can be ridden by a witch for a magical purpose. Besides, the earth tides and the seasons change us, our spirits and bodies respond to them. Knowing this, we can use the sabbats to come into an increasing harmony with what is actually happening in nature. For instance, we can use the winter season as a time of contemplation and inwardness, making plans, dreaming the future, and summer, when nature is active and creative, for more intense making, doing and adventuring.

Most of the festivals are marked in public ways, by people other than witches. They are an ancestral matter for everyone, and are of our native European tradition, predating Christianity. The Church has arranged many of its own holy days to coincide with these ancient festivals, and in Britain there are secular holidays (bank holidays) around or near Beltane and Lughnasadh. Also, there are many folk customs, known to everybody, which derive from Pagan concepts connected with the sabbats – for example, the maypole dances at Beltane and 'ducking for apples' at Hallowe'en (Samhain).

The entire set of eight sabbats do not seem to have had equal importance to all our ancestors. The Celts favored the greater sabbats, while the Saxons seem to have liked the celebrations of solstices and equinoxes. The builders of the megaliths laid much emphasis upon the solstices, but also, on the evidence of folk belief, upon the greater sabbats. Modern Pagans, liking the symmetry of the eight-spoked 'wheel of the year', tend to give equal importance to all of them.

Sometimes, the Moon's phases are linked with the celebration of sabbats, so that the festival will be marked on the nearest full moon to the usual date. However, the solstices and equinoxes happen precisely in accordance with the Sun's position. As most people know, the winter solstice is the occasion of the year's longest night (in the northern hemisphere). The summer solstice is the longest day. And, at each equinox, day and night are equal in length. None of these events has anything to do with the Sun's entry into particular zodiacal signs. It is a common fallacy that, for instance, the winter solstice occurs when the Sun enters Capricorn. Sometimes it may, but not necessarily. The lesser sabbats are actually caused by the Sun's declination, to the north or south of the equator.

All the eight festivals (together as a set) express the annual cycle of the Earth in relation to the Sun. Paganism teaches that we can go with these great natural cycles, and enjoy increasing inner harmony, good health and fruitful magic, or ignore them, and so live in alienation from natural rhythms, to our own undoing. In a culture that is moving toward twenty-four-hour shops, at all times of the year, and has come to rely on imported, unseasonal fruits and vegetables, this is not a popular message. However, the truth remains that attempting to live in accord with natural cycles is a major spiritual practice, acknowledged by Pagans all over the globe, from Druids to Taoists to American Indians.

Each one of the sabbats has a link with all three realms of the world tree. The upperworld, obviously, is in focus because of the Sun. (Since many people celebrate sabbats at night, it is often visually evident to us that, in fact, the Moon's phase and the entire astrological picture, and even the rising or setting of some constellations, are also factors within any specific festival.) Even more obvious is the middle Earth aspect, since nature spirits live with and by seasons. As for the underworld, that is felt strongly. All the sabbats are known to be times when the faerie presences do come among us. It is clear that they are all portals to the underworld (some sabbats more strongly than others, but all to some extent). However, the emphasis at any festival is very much upon what is happening in nature, in middle Earth. All our rites and spells arise from and are shaped by that, which is good, because Earth is where we are. What it all comes back down to, in the end, is how we live on the Earth.

Some suggested prayers for the sabbats are as follows.

Imbolg – February

Themes – Purification and inspiration. In nature, we see spring floods in water meadows. Rivers and brooks run high. The remains of last year's vegetation are rotted down, to prepare the ground for new growth. The land, sodden and muddy, is literally being washed and made fresh again. The first spring leaves and flowers appear – snowdrops, dog's mercury and winter aconite. Alder and hazel may come into blossom. There are newborn lambs. Beginning. Freshening. The growth of light and the lengthening of the days. A new start.

Imbolg Prayer

> *Great Lady and Lord of the year's dawn, the new light that washes us, first stirrings of the light, I call upon you. Bless this land, bless streams and rivers, bless hills and valleys, bless fields and forests. As all is pure and clear, stripped down for new growth, so may our lives be made ready for new creativity.*

*Inspire us to celebrate the land's beauty and mystery
– and all of life.*

The above prayer may seem much easier to say if you live in
the country. However, wildwood mysticism is rooted in
nature, and we witches must take our cue from signs in parks
or gardens, or from the sight of our rivers that roll through
the cities, when living far from open country.

If you live in the southern hemisphere, you will, of course
be saying this prayer in early August. In fact, all the rites for
the sabbats will be held on opposite times of the year to those
of the northern hemisphere. Wherever you live, please adapt
this prayer to your own local climate and conditions, still
concentrating on the idea of freshness, beginnings.

Suggested Spells

Middle Earth – Traditionally, this is the time of the year for
spring cleaning. Any clearing of cupboards or giving of
unwanted clothes to charity shops, or bottles to the bottle
dump, may be done with ritual significance. It may be consecrated to 'clearing the ground' in preparation for a new life
for yourself. But also, it may be dedicated to the principle of
recycling, as a spell for the environment.

Underworld – Visit a holy well or spring. If possible, bathe
your eyes with the water and make a request to the faeries to
show you the way forward in the coming year.

Upperworld – Light three candles, as is traditional at Imbolg.
With the first, make a wish that humanity receive fresh inspiration about how to live at peace with all other species. With
the second, make a wish that new, environmentally sound
technology become widespread, replacing what is destructive. With the third, wish for the healing of the human spirit.

Eostre/Spring Equinox – 21 March

Themes – A new fertility. Emerging. A different balance (day and night are equal at the spring equinox but from now on the light will increase over darkness). Named for the Saxon Goddess Eostre, this is the time for resurgence in every way, but especially of fertility. Chicks hatch out, coming from darkness (inside the egg) into light. Rabbits (or, more traditionally, hares or nowadays, 'Easter bunnies') are the symbol of new fertility, a renewed self, an emerging into the light, like a daffodil from the earth.

Spring Equinox Prayer

Great Lady and Lord of all fecund life, renewed strength and joyful, young creatures, I now invoke you. Bless the young of all wild animals, struggling to survive. Grant them protection. Bless all the people and renew our spirits, in love. Renew our true understanding of our native spiritual heritage. And make our souls fertile, that we become rich with new tales to live by, new poems and songs, that interpret the ancient wisdom, for now and always.

Suggested Spells

Middle Earth – Bring daffodils or any bright spring flowers into your home. Dedicate them with the following words: *As these flowers fill this place with scent and color, so may vibrant, joyful strength increase in all who live here.* This is a good spell to do following any late winter illness, like a bout of flu.

Underworld – Paint an egg with symbols that denote the kind of fertility you would like to see. For example, for an increase in woodland, paint a miniature tree, or leaves. If you would like to see an increase in kindness between people, paint a stylized heart. An increase in witchcraft? Paint pentagrams. When the design is dry, place the egg upon your altar for a day and a night. Then lay it on the earth, with a prayer to the faeries.

Upperworld – Light a fire to the Sun, with an invocation that as the Sun grows in strength through the summer, so shall the human spirit be renewed in love.

Beltane (May Eve) – 30 April

Themes – Blossoming. Desire. Love. Union. This is the festival of love. Our ancestors danced around maypoles at this time, which represented the male (the pole: phallus) entwined with the female (the ribbons: vulva). Symbolically, and actually, this sabbat is about the dance of love. People used to go out into the greenwood on May Eve to make love – and still do – in remote places. This celebrates the union between the Goddess and God, who create all life. The theme is the union of opposites. One gender or project or element marrying with another, for a more creative result.

Beltane Prayer

> *Great Lady and Lord of the greenwood marriage bed, you who bless joyful desire, I call upon you. Bless lovers everywhere with true fulfillment. Bless wild love and romance and passion. Let us all blossom out in our lives, and dare to love without reserve, and yet with wisdom. But heal all those who have loved unrequitedly. Let none be left without a partner within the spiral dance. Whether in the spirit*

or the body, let all be at one with a true beloved, from now on.

This prayer does not seem to leave much room for the choice of celibacy. However, as the last sentence implies, a relationship that is of the spirit alone may be the real romance, for those whose soul mates are not now incarnate. Traditionally, this festival really does celebrate joyful sex – but the concept may be taken poetically to mean any loving union, on any level.

Suggested spells

Middle Earth – Make a small maypole, about the size of a wand (that is, approximately the length of your elbow to your finger tips). The best wood to use is birch. Consecrate the maypole wand to represent your creative will. Take three ribbons of a colour that symbolizes what you most desire. For instance, pink for love, green for a country life, red for renewed health and vigour etc. Attach them to the top of the wand. Then 'marry' the ribbons and wand, by twisting the ribbons around the wand and around each other. Say, *So may my dream of _____ [e.g. love] come true, and my will serve that _____ [love, health, or whatever you want] and my life be made new. So may it be.* Leave the ribbons bound around the wand. Put the whole thing in a safe place.

Underworld – Beltane's greenwood marriage theme has a subtext. It says that sometimes we must go beyond safe boundaries (out into the greenwood, beyond the village or town) for the sake of what is sacred or for love. We may have to flout convention, in order to uphold a principle or a relationship. Like the outlaws of old, we may need, symbolically, to take to the forest. Beltane is therefore a good time to walk in the woods and, after finding a suitable quiet glade, to swear fidelity to the craft of the witch, with your hand on a tree. Or to vow allegiance with all those who uphold the principles that you hold most dear, whether these are environmental, social, political or spiritual. Ask the faeries to bear witness and to keep you to this oath. (If you are going to the green-wood for the sake of a relationship, then, of course, the two of you should go together and make vows to each other.)

Upperworld – Write a poem describing the sacred nature of sexual and romantic love. Tie it to a tree and leave it there overnight, with a prayer to the deities to change all human minds about love – from ideas of shame, abuse, guilt, exploitation and degradation to knowledge of holiness, magic, the life force and tenderness. The night breeze will waft your words upward.

Litha/Summer Solstice – 21 June

Themes – Beauty, fulfillment. The power of happiness to change our lives. Also, dedication, commitment. The Sun is now radiant! In the whole year, this is the time of the greatest light in the northern hemisphere. There is great celebration, for life is good. People play music. Some stay out in the fields all night, with friends or lovers. The time has come to live fully. At the summer solstice (as at any high point of life, any peak of fulfillment) we can be changed by the experience of joyfulness, by the land's loveliness or by a healing vision of how harmony could be restored to all beings – and decide to serve that vision. As with any climax, this is a turning point. Things will be differ-ent now. What we distill from the year's culmination will enrich our spirits and affect our future creative direction.

Summer Solstice Prayer

   Great Lady and Lord of the golden Sun and golden

*days on Earth and the heart's fulfillment, I call upon
you. Let all be blessed with a sense of the beauty of
this Earth and all her creatures. Help us to celebrate
love for one another and for all life. And help us also
to put to flight forces that oppress love and deny
justice. Make us strong in magic. Make us like
summer trees. Make us like summer stars. Make us
like summer seas. In dedication to the vision of
untamed peace, set us free.*

Suggested Spells

Middle Earth – Throw a party and dedicate it to increased
fun, celebration and enjoyment for yourself and all your
friends – a party dedicated to the spirit of joyful freedom. Or
perhaps a small dinner party for two, consecrated to future
happiness.

Underworld – If your life lacks happiness or you feel alone,
anoint yourself with rose oil and ask the faeries to bring you
the fulfillment that you need, whether this be a new romance,
more friends or just a better relationship with life generally.

Upperworld, middle Earth and underworld (all at once)
– This festival has been linked with the Pagan Grail, that
heals the wasteland – the Celtic cauldron of regeneration
which restores life to a deadened heart or a damaged environment. Take a chalice of wine. Any ordinary wine glass
or chalice-shaped container will do for this, whether of glass
or pottery or wood or metal. Breathe into it a long description of the Earth in her beauty. This need not be difficult.
You can say things like, *Trees that are strong and green
and healthy, wildflowers everywhere, foxes, hares,
badgers, deer, skylarks and thrushes and clear, clean
rivers and strong fishes*, and so on. You can alter this, if

necessary, to describe the beauty of your area or land. When you have poured your words into the wine, so that it is imbued with all those images, say,

> *Let this be the way on Earth.*
> *Let this be.*
> *Wild creatures and plants and places*
> *in regeneration.*
> *Wild and free and strong and everywhere!*

Take three sips, then pour the rest out on the ground, saying, *I give this vision to life. May we all share it and live by it.*

Lughnasadh/Lammas – 1 August

Themes – The first fruits of Harvest. The promise of what is to come, when all is gathered in, is evident in the hedgerows and fields now. Bread from wheat – thus, transformation. Mourning within the thanksgiving (the Sun declines in strength and days will get shorter now). To gather in all the crops, we must work. Giving of ourselves our own time and energy. This is true in our lives as well as in the fields, so there is a theme of sacrifice at Lughhasadh. What would we give to make sure that our lives bear fruit and that all mouths are fed, in a just, harmonious world?

Lughnasadh Prayer

> *Great Lady and Lord of the first fruits of Harvest –*
> *blackberry, strawberry, crabapple – I call to you.*
> *Goddess and God of the good wheat, oats and barley,*
> *and all the ripening orchards, I now invoke you.*
> *Thank you for all blessings. Thank you for all*
> *harvests, throughout the realms, everywhere. May all*

be gathered in safely. Bless every farmer who treats the land with respect. May such be granted good fortune. We offer care for the Earth and her creatures. Let this increase in us.

Suggested Spells

Middle Earth – Take a loaf or roll of organic bread. Place one hand upon it. Say, *I bless, consecrate and set apart this bread, in the names of the Great Mother Goddess and the Father God. May it serve as a symbol of all nourishment. As I eat it, may all be fed with good food of all kinds. Let none go hungry. And, as I give it back to Earth, our mother, may she and all creatures thrive.*

Eat some of the bread and then crumble the rest on the garden or in the fields. The use of organic bread is, of course, an invocation for the people to be fed with natural foods of good quality, and for organic goods to be produced widely. Visualize that this is occurring. See the Earth Mother relaxing, in consequence, song birds returning to the farmland, the people healthier.

Underworld – Take a piece of fruit. Consecrate it to represent some aspect of yourself e.g. your creativity, strength or magical power. Bury it in the earth, with a prayer to the deities that it be accepted, in the service of life. You can be quite specific and say, for example, *May my artistic ability serve nature conservation*, or *May my magical strength serve the cause of healing*. Whatever you wish. From now on, that aspect of yourself will change, becoming what it needs to be, to serve your chosen cause. Burial always implies a resurrection, in magical terms. The spell will result in a reborn version of your gift.

Upperworld – Take a cloth and cover a clear glass bowl

containing water. Position it out in the open fields or in the garden, beneath the full moon that is nearest to Lughnasadh. Say, *As the Moon shines on the water, so may the people of this land be blessed with a vision of how we may live in real harmony, with the Earth and one another.* Remove the cloth. Tilt the bowl, if necessary, so that the moonlight can be seen, reflected. Then pour out the water upon the ground.

Mabon/Autumn Equinox – 21 September

Themes – Harvest festival. Thanksgiving for the complete harvest, now all is gathered in. The scales of balance. Day and night are of equal length, as at the spring equinox, but from now on, the dark will be gaining. We weigh up the gains of our year, or of our lives, as against the losses. We celebrate the gains, for these are not only our sustenance for the future, but also hold the seeds which will be planted for the next cycle of growth. With the losses, we take time to come to terms and learn by our mistakes. The autumn equinox helps us to understand how we may cope with 'a moment of reckoning'.

Autumn Equinox Prayer

> *Great Lady and Lord of abundance and of the scales of justice, I now invoke you. Food, clothing, shelter, love and creativity are your gifts to us, and we give thanks. Now the harvest of grain is all gathered. In our lives, too, the year's gifts have been received. Help us to clearly distinguish between chaff and seed in our personal harvest. To recognize what we've really got or have not. And, as we turn inward, toward the dark season of winter, may all be blessed.*

May all receive, each according to their need, in fairness.

Suggested Spells

Middle Earth – Make or buy a corn dolly. Hang it up indoors, with a prayer to the Goddess and God to bless your home with continuing health and prosperity, throughout the winter.

Underworld – Drink blackberry wine, or eat blackberries, with a prayer to the underworld deities to strengthen your contact with the faeries. Blackberries were once believed to be the faeries' fruit. If you ate them, especially outside, by a blackberry bush, you could be carried off to the otherworld. You've been warned!

Upperworld – Make a commitment to feed the wild birds, all through the winter. Many once common birds, like song thrushes, are now endangered species. The numbers of most types of garden birds have dropped enormously. To feed them is an offering, a giving back to the powers of nature, from our own harvest.

Samhain/Hallowe'en – 31 October

Themes – Death and rebirth. Sap has sunk down to the roots of the trees and the year's growth is at an end in this land. It is the start of winter. In Europe, this is the Festival of the Dead. At this time, our forebears communed with the ancestors, and received guidance, as do modern Pagans. We may also sense the unborn, those who will enter our lives as children or grandchildren. This is traditionally a time for divination, about future lovers or partners. The major theme of this day is that death is a beginning. It is the first stage in the transition toward a new cycle of life. Accordingly, the Celts named Samhain as the first day of the New Year. It is also a time when the 'veils' are said to be at their thinest, between the spirit realm and the mortal world.

Samhain Prayer

Great Goddess and God of the spirit realms, I call upon you. Now, at this time of mist and bonfires and spirit presences, we celebrate the dead. Help us all remember loved friends and relatives who have died, and sense their love for us. Help us all to hear their advice and guidance, and that of the more distant ancestors, who are the guardians of ancient wisdom. We know that you preside within an otherworld of boundless beauty, where the dead rest between lives. May we find that place within us, the land of the summer stars. For it is from there that we may be reborn, more wise and free, in strength and beauty.

Suggested Spells

Middle Earth – Since this is the time of death and transformation, write in red ink on a piece of paper whatever you wish to banish from your own life, or from your community. For instance, bad health or greed. Burn the paper in a candle flame, with the words, *As this paper burns, so may what is written upon it be gone from the world, with harm to none. May the spirit of it be transformed. So may it be reborn as harmony, in wisdom.*

This spell is commonly known and widely used among witches because it works. It is vital to use it only to banish bad qualities or unpleasant attitudes. The use of it to banish a person from a particular situation, for example, could be manipulative and would undoubtedly invoke the law of three-fold return, which would mean the spellcaster, her or himself, would get banished, eventually.

Underworld – Light a candle. Say, *In the name of the Lady and Lord of the spirit realms, I welcome the beloved dead around this flame.*

Spend time remembering dead relatives or friends. Name each one, calling them in (if they wish to come). Speak to them in your mind, thanking them for all the good times you shared, or for anything that they taught you, when they were alive. Say anything that you want to say, especially if there is any issue that you didn't get the chance to explain about before their death. Ask if they have any messages or advice for you, or anything at all that they want you to hear. Sit quietly now. You may see images with your inner sight, or hear something, with your 'mind's ear'. When you are ready, say to them, *Hail and farewell, with my blessing.* If you wish, you may add the traditional witches' valediction, *Merry meet and merry part and merry meet again.*

Upperworld – Sit or lie in complete darkness. If necessary, cover your head with a shawl or a blanket, to block out any light from your candles. If outdoors in the country, simply sit under the stars and close your eyes. Visualize (or describe to yourself) a black void, as at the beginning of the world. A black empty firmament. Nothingness. Now see stars begin-ning to shine, one by one – and then whole galaxies – and then the planets – the Earth, brand new. Visualize the whole passage of aeons, the mud and ferns and dinosaurs, the new appearance of flowers, trees, animals, continents arising, changing. Now see the people – the most complex animal – learning and making mistakes and relearning, and in the end, achieving wisdom. A world of harmony, people at one with Earth, adventurous and yet peaceful. Technology that is based on renewable resources. No more wars, because we have developed magical and psychological and legal strategies to avert them. Tolerance for every religion, race and type. In fact, a great celebration of our diversity. Treasuring of the Earth's beauty and wildness and all her most sacred places. An honoring of all people who have special magical or psychic skills. A new relationship between the human and faerie realms.

Say, *So may this be*, and open your eyes again, knowing you have dreamt the world awake.

Yule/Winter Solstice – 21 December

Themes – Birth. The turning of the wheel of the seasons, from dark to light. The Sun's rebirth. Trees hung with lights. Peace and goodwill (the Celts ordained a twelve-day cessation of all conflicts, at Midwinter Festival – it was a time when all fighting was forbidden). A new cycle of life and a new dispensation, symbolized as a newborn child. A time to honor the Mother Goddess and the fact of motherhood – traditionally, most people return to their mother's home at some time during the twelve days of the Yule celebration. The Goddess's gift of a new start, that promise fulfilled.

Winter Solstice Prayer

> *Great Lady and Lord of the turning wheel of the year's seasons, by whom the light returns, I call to you. Now, at the darkest time, when all of nature is still and cold, the change is made. There is a pause, as though between breaths, all nature waits, and then – the dawn comes early! There is rebirth of light and we begin again. Let hope and joyfulness be reborn, therefore, in all hearts. And let none be lonely. Let*

all see, as new light grows, how we may live peace-
fully and in shared happiness. Let war cease. Let us
make a world fit for children.

Suggested Spells

Middle Earth – Make a Yule wreath. As you do so, visualize the evergreen plants you are using as symbolic of the thread of life, continuing even in the darkest times. Weave into the wreath your hopes for the future and for the survival of threatened species.

Underworld – Invoke the faerie goddessmothers, who bless and protect all newborn hopes and gifts, as well as all newborn babies. Place offerings of food and drink for them upon your dinner table. Open the door wide to welcome them to your home, with a request that they bless any good new idea or project, as well as the children of the house (in fact anything that is new or young) for the coming year.

Upperworld – Light a candle to the rebirth of the Sun, with the words, *As this flame burns, may the light of* ____ [e.g. renewed Pagan worship or religious tolerance] *burn brightly, illuminating the world for all children. And may the great Sun, to whom this flame is dedicated, ensure that the spell shines on, increasing.*

Well, those are the eight sabbats, the spokes of the wheel of the witch's year. The prayers I have given are suggestions only, as are the spells. In time, you will want to create your own, based upon the themes of the festivals. With the help of your familiars, and with a clear observation of nature's patterns, you can soon develop new ways of using the old knowledge, that are in keeping with today's world.

Remember, a wildwood mystic is a kind of explorer, as well

as a priestess or priest of the ancient deities. We look back to the oldest traditions and – surprise! – they are new, awaiting discovery. Our awareness of mystery, in stone and flower, sea and star and in all the creatures, is always a new experience, inviting us to find fresh ways of fate weaving. To discover magic. So – wise and blessed be, because a hedge witch's prayer book is not a fixed, final document. Instead, it is something all witches create, remake and add to, continuously. It is stored in the spirit realm, in memory. It is found inside hazelnuts or underneath the sea or spelled out by flights of birds, to name a few ways of reading it. It is scanned easily by moonlight, but can be heard, anytime, carried on the wind. Thus, wildwood mystics, the hedge witches, are both bound (by laws of nature and of life) and free, within the old traditions.

Bibliography

Anderson, William, *Green Man: The Archetype of Our Oneness with the Earth* (HarperCollins, 1990)

Beth, Rae, *Hedge Witch* (Robert Hale, 1990)

____, *The Wiccan Path* (The Crossing Press, Inc., 1995)

____, *Lamp of the Goddess* (Robert Hale, 1994) (formerly titled *Reincarnation and the Dark Goddess*)

Evans-Wentz, W.Y., *The Fairy-Faith in Celtic Countries*, new edn (Dufour Editions, 1992)

Farrar, Janet and Stewart, *The Witches' Way* (Phoenix Publishing Inc., 1984)

Franklin, Anna, *Familiars* (Capall Bann, 1997)

Lavender, Susan & Anna Franklin, *Herb Craft* (Capall Bann, 1996)

James, Catrin, *Celtic Faery Shamanism* (Capall Bann, 1998)

____, *Celtic Faery Shamanism Volume Two: The Wisdom of the Otherworld* (Capall Bann, 1999)

Jones, Kathy, *In the Nature of Avalon: Goddess Pilgrimages in Glastonbury's Sacred Landscape* (Ariadne Publications, 2000)

Mathews, Caitlin, *Singing the Soul Back Home: Shamanism in Daily Life* (Element Books, 1995)

Mynne, Hugh, *The Faery Way* (Llewellyn Publications, 1996)

Palin, Poppy, *Season of Sorcery: On Becoming a Wise-woman* (Capall Bann, 1998)

____, *Wildwitch: The Craft of the Natural Psychic* (Capall

Bann, 1999)

Paterson, Jacqueline Memory, *Tree Wisdom* (Thorsons, 1996)

Potter, Chesca, *The Greenwood Tarot Handbook* (Sacred Sight Publications, 1998)

Robertson, Olivia, *Maya: Goddess Rites for Solo Use* (Cesara Publications) (Also, the following books: *Dea*; *Panthea*; *Psyche*; *Sophia*; *Sybil*; *Urania*)

Smith, Jill, *The Callanish Dance* (Capall Bann, 2000)

Stewart, R.J., *Earthlight: Rediscovering the Wisdom of Celtic and Faery Lore* (Element Books, 1992)

____, *The Living World of Faery* (Mercury Publishing, 1999)

Addresses

THE PAGAN FEDERATION
BM Box 7097
LONDON WC1N 3XX
www.paganfed.demon.co.uk

THE FELLOWSHIP OF ISIS (inc. Cesara Publications)
The Hon. Olivia Robertson
Clonegal Castle
Enniscorthy
Co. Wexford
Eire
www.fellowshipofisis.com

Rae Beth
www.raebeth.net